# Arguments of Celsus, Porphyry, and the Emperor Julian, Against the Christians

P. G. Wodehouse

**Arguments of Celsus, Porphyry, and the Emperor Julian, Against the Christians**

The present edition is a reproduction of previous publication of this classic work. Minor typographical errors may have been corrected without note, however, for an authentic reading experience the spelling, punctuation, and capitalization have been retained from the original text.

ISBN: 978-1-64799-149-4

# CONTENTS

## BY THOMAS TAYLOR

## MDCCCXXX

"For if indeed Julian had caused all those that were under his dominion to be richer than Midas, and each of the cities greater than Babylon once was, and had also surrounded each of them with a golden wall, but had corrected none of the existing errors respecting divinity, he would have acted in a manner similar to a physician, who receiving a body full of evils in each of its parts, should cure all of them except the eyes."—

Liban. Parental, in Julian, p. 285

# INTRODUCTION

"I HAVE often wished," says Warburton in a letter to Dr. Forster, October 15, 1749, "for a hand capable of collecting all the fragments remaining of Porphyry, Celsus, Hierocles, and Julian, and giving them to us with a just, critical and theological comment, as a defy to infidelity. It is certain we want something more than what their ancient answerers have given us. This would be a very noble work[1]."

The author of the following Collectanea has partially effected what Dr. Warburton wished to see accomplished; for as he is not a divine, he has not attempted in his Notes to confute Celsus, but has confined himself solely to an illustration of his meaning, by a citation of parallel passages in other ancient authors.

As the answer, however, of Origen to the arguments of Celsus is very futile and inefficient, it would be admirable to see some one of the learned divines with which the church at present abounds, leap into the arena, and by vanquishing Celsus, prove that the Christian religion is peculiarly adapted to the present times, and to the interest of the priests by whom it is professed and disseminated.

---

[1] See Barker's Parriana, vol. ii. p. 48.

The Marquis D'Argens published a translation in French, accompanied by the Greek text, of the arguments of the Emperor Julian against the Christians; and as an apology for the present work, I subjoin the following translation of a part of his preliminary discourse, in which he defends that publication.

"It may be that certain half-witted gentleman may reproach me for having brought forward a work composed in former times against the Christians, in the vulgar tongue. To such I might at once simply reply, that the work was preserved by a Father of the Church; but I will go further, and tell them with Father Petau, who gave a Greek edition of the works of Julian, that if those who condemn the authors that have published these works, will temper the ardour of their zeal with reason and judgement, they will think differently, and will distinguish between the good use that may be made of the book, and the bad intentions of the writer.

"Father Petau also judiciously remarks, that if the times were not gone by when dæmons took the advantage of idolatry to seduce mankind, it would be prudent not to afford any aid, or give the benefit of any invective against Jesus, or the Christian religion to the organs of those dæmons; but since by the blessing of God and the help of the cross, which have brought about our salvation, the monstrous dogmas of Paganism are buried in oblivion, we have nothing to fear from that pest; there is no weighty reason for our rising up against the monuments of Pagan aberration that now remain, and totally destroying them. On the contrary, the same Father Petau says, that it is better to treat them as the ancient Christians treated the images and temples of the gods. At first, in the provinces in which they were in power, they razed them to the very foundations, that nothing might be visible to posterity that could perpetuate impiety, or the sight of which could recall mankind to an abominable worship. But when the same Christians had firmly established their religion, it appeared more rational to them, after destroying the altars and statues of the gods, to preserve the temples, and by purifying them, to make them serviceable for the worship of the true God. The same Christians also, not only discontinued to break the statues and images of the gods, but they took the choicest of them, that were the work of the most celebrated artists, and set them up in public places to ornament their cities, as well as to recall to the memory of those who beheld them, how gross the blindness[2] of their ancestors had been, and how powerful the grace that had delivered them from it."

The Marquis d'Argens further observes: "It were to be wished, that Father Petau, having so judiciously considered the works of Julian, had formed an equally correct idea of the person of that Emperor. I cannot discover through what caprice he takes it amiss, that a certain learned Professor[3] has praised the civil virtues of Julian, and condemned the evidently false calumnies that almost all the ecclesiastical authors have lavished upon him; and amongst the rest Gregory and Cyril, who to the good arguments they have adduced against the false reasoning of Julian, have added insults which ought never to have been used by any defender of truth. They have cruelly calumniated this Emperor to favour their good cause, and confounded the just, wise, clement, and most courageous prince, with the Pagan philosopher and theologian; when they ought simply to have refuted him with argument, in no case with insult,

---

[2] The Heathens would here reply to Father Petau. Which is the greater blindness of the two, — ours, in worshipping the images of deiform processions from the ineffable principle of things, and who are eternally united to him; or that of the Papists, in worshipping the images of worthless men.

[3] Monsieur de la Bletric.

vii

and still less with calumnies so evidently false, that during fourteen centuries, in which they have been so often repeated, they have never been accredited, nor enabled to assume even an air of truth."

A wise Christian philosopher, La Mothe, Le Vayer, in reflecting on the great virtues with which Julian was endowed, on the contempt he manifested for death, on the firmness with which he consoled those who wept around him, and on his last conversation with Maximus and Priscus on the immortality of the soul, says, "that after such testimonies of a virtue, to which nothing appears to be wanting but the faith to give its professor a place amongst the blessed[4], we have cause to wonder that Heathens that lived posterior, but those also who lived anterior to the promulgation of the Christian religion, will have no place hereafter among the blessed.

Cyril should have tried to make us believe, that Julian was a mean and cowardly prince[5]. Those who judge of men that lived in former ages by those who have lived in more recent times, may feel little surprise at the proceedings of Cyril. It has rarely happened that long animosity and abuse have not been introduced into religious controversies."

After what has been above said of Julian, I deem it necessary to observe, that Father Petau is egregiously mistaken in supposing that Cyril has preserved the whole of that Emperor's arguments

---

[4] According to this wise Christian philosopher therefore, not only all the confessedly wise and virtuous.

[5] This is by no means wonderful in Cyril, when we consider that he is, with the strongest reason, suspected of being the cause of the murder of Hypatia, who was one of the brightest ornaments of the Alexandrian school, and who was not only a prodigy of learning, but also a paragon of beauty.

against the Christians: and the Marquis D'Argêns is also mistaken when he says, that "the passages of Julian's text which are abridged or omitted, aire very few." For Hieronymus in Epist. 83. Ad Magnum Oratorem Romanum, testifies that this work consisted of seven books; three of which only Cyril attempted to confute, as is evident from his own words, [—Greek—] "Julian wrote three books against the holy Evangelists." But as Fabricius observes, (in Biblioth. Græc. tom. vii. p. 89.) in the other four books, he appears to have attacked the remaining books of the Scriptures, i. e. the books of the Old Testament.

With respect, however, to the three books which Cyril has endeavoured to confute, it appears to me, that he has only selected such parts of these books as he thought he could most easily answer. For that he has not given even the substance of these three books, is evident from the words of Julian himself, as recorded by Cyril. For Julian, after certain invectives both against Christ and John, says, "These things, therefore, we shall shortly discuss, when we come particularly to consider the monstrous deeds and fraudulent machinations of the Evangelists[6]." There is no particular discussion however of these in any part of the extracts preserved by Cyril.

That the work, indeed, of Julian against the Christians was of considerable extent, is evident from the testimony of his contemporary, Libanius; who, in his admirable funeral oration on this most extraordinary man, has the following remarkable passage: "But when the winter had extended the nights, Julian, besides many other beautiful works, attacked the books which make a man of Palestine to be a God, and the son of God; and in a long contest, and

---

[6] [—Greek—]

with strenuous arguments, evinced that what is said in these writings is ridiculous and nugatory. And in the execution of this work he appears to have excelled in wisdom the Tyrian old man.[7]

In asserting this however, may the Tyrian be propitious to me, and benevolently receive what I have said, he having been vanquished by his son[8]."

With respect to Celsus, the author of the following Fragments, he lived in the time of the Emperor Adrian and was, if Origen may be credited, an Epicurean philosopher. That he might indeed, at some former period of his life, have been an Epicurean maybe admitted; but it would be highly absurd to suppose that he was so when he wrote this invective against the Christians; for the arguments which he mostly employs show that he was well skilled m the philosophy of Plato: and to suppose, as Origen does, that he availed himself of arguments in which he did not believe, and consequently conceived to be erroneous, in order to confute doctrines which he was persuaded are false, would be to make him, instead of a philosopher, a fool. As to Origen, though he abandoned philosophy for Christianity, he was considered as heterodox by many of the Christian sect. Hence, with some of the Catholics, his future salvation became a matter of doubt[9]; and this induced the celebrated Johannes Picus Mirandulanus, in the last of his Theological conclusions according to his own opinion, to say:

---

[7]    viz. Porphyry, who was of Tyre, and who, as is well known, wrote a work against the Christians, which was publicly burnt by order of the Emperor Constantine.

[8] [—Greek—]

[9] 'In Prato Spiritual!, c. 26, quod citatur, à VIL Synodo, et à Johanne Diacono, lib. ii. c. 45. vitas B. Gregorii narratur fevelatio, qua Origines viras est in Gehenna ignis cum Alio et Netftorio."*—Fobric. BMiotk Grate torn. v. p. 216

"Rationabilius est credere Uriginem esse salvum, quam credere ipsum esse damnatum," i. e. It is more reasonable to believe that Origen is saved, than that he is damned.

I shall conclude this Introduction with the following extract.

## Directions of Dr. Barlow, Bishop of Lincoln, to a young divine

"It will be of great use for a divine to be acquainted with the arts, knavery, and fraud of the Roman inquisitor, in purging, correcting, or rather corrupting authors in all arts and faculties. For this purpose we may consult the Index Expurgatorius. By considering this Index, we come to know the best editions of many good books.

"1st. The best books; that is, those that are condemned.

"2nd. The best editions; viz. those that are dated before the Index, and consequently not altered.

"3rd. The Index is a good common place book, to point out who has written well against the Church, p. 70.

"Ockam is damned in the Index, and therefore we may be sure he was guilty of telling some great truth, p. 41.[10]"

---

[10] The Bishop's rule is as good for one church as for another, and every church has its Index.

# THE ARGUMENTS OF CELSUS AGAINST THE CHRISTIANS

"THE Christians are accustomed to have private assemblies, which are forbidden by the law. For of assemblies some are public, and these are conformable to the law of the land; but others are secret, and these are such as are hostile to the laws; among which are the Love Feasts of the Christians[11].

---

[11] Why the Romans punished the Christians:

"It is commonly regarded as a very curious and remarkable fact, that, although the Romans were disposed to tolerate every other religious sect, yet they frequently persecuted the Christians with unrelenting cruelty. This exception, so fatal to a peaceable and harmless sect, must have originated in circumstances which materially distin guished them from the votaries of every other religion. The causes and the pretexts of persecution may have varied at various periods; but there seems to have been one general cause which will readily be apprehended by those who are intimately acquainted with the Roman jurisprudence. From the most remote period of their history, the Romans had conceived extreme horror against all nocturnal meetings of a secret and mysterious nature. A law prohibiting nightly vigils in a temple has even been ascribed, perhaps with little probability, to the founder of their state. The laws of the twelve tables declared it a capital offence to attend nocturnal assemblies in the city. This, then, being the spirit of the law, it is obvious that the nocturnal meetings

1

"Men who irrationally assent to anything, resemble those who are delighted with jugglers and enchanters, &c. For as most of these are depraved characters, who deceive the vulgar, and persuade them to assent to whatever they please, this also takes place with the Christians. Some of these are not willing either to give or receive a reason for what they believe; but are accustomed to say, 'Do not investigate, but believe, your faith will save you.

'For the wisdom of the world is bad, but folly is good[12],'

"The world, according to Moses, was created at a certain time, and has from its commencement existed for a period far short of ten thousand years,—The world, however, is without a beginning; in consequence of which there have been from all eternity many

---

of the primitive Christians must have rendered them objects of peculiar suspicion, and exposed them to the animadversion of the magistrate. It was during the night that they usually held their most solemn and religious assemblies; for a practice which may be supposed to have arisen from their fears, seems to have been continued from the operation of other causes. Misunderstanding the purport of certain passages of Scripture, they were led to imagine that the second advent, of which they lived in constant expectation, would take place during the night; and they were accustomed to celebrate nightly vigils at the tombs of the saints and martyrs. In this case, therefore, they incurred no penalties peculiar to the votaries of a new religion, but only such as equally attached to those who, professing the public religion of the state, were yet guilty of this undoubted violation of its laws."—Observations on the Study of the Civil Law, by Dr. Irving, Edin. 1820. p. 11.

"It is not true that the primitive Christians held their assemblies in the night time to avoid the interruptions of the civil power: but the converse of that proposition is true in the utmost latitude; viz. that they met with molestations from that quarter, because their assemblies were nocturnal."—Elements of Civil Law, by Dr. Taylor, p. 579.

[12] See Erasmus's Praise of Folly, towards the end.

conflagrations, and many deluges, among the latter of which the most recent is that of Deucalion[13].

"Goatherds and shepherds among the Jews, following Moses as their leader, and being allured by rustic deceptions, conceived that there is [only] one God.

"These goatherds and shepherds were of opinion that there is one God, whether they delight to call him the Most High, or Adonai, or Celestial, or Sabaoth, or to celebrate by any other name the fabricator of this world[14]; for they knew nothing farther. For it is of no consequence, whether the God who is above all things, is denominated, after the accustomed manner of the Greeks, Jupiter, or is called by any other name, such as that which is given to him by the Indians or Egyptians."

Celsus, assuming the person of a Jew, represents him as speaking to Jesus, and reprehending him for many things. And in the first place he reproaches him with feigning that he was born of a virgin; and says, that to his disgrace he was born in a Judaic village from a poor Jewess, who obtained the means of subsistence by manual labour. He adds, That she was abandoned by her husband, who was a carpenter, because she had been found by him to have committed adultery. Hence, in consequence of being expelled by her husband, becoming an ignominious vagabond, she was secretly delivered of Jesus, who, through poverty being obliged to serve as a hireling in Egypt, learnt there certain arts for which the Egyptians are famous.

---

[13] See on this subject the Tinusus of Plato.
[14] In the original there is nothing more than [−Greek−] i. e. this world; but it is necessary to read, conformably to the above translation, [−Greek−]. For the Jews did not celebrate the world, but the Maker of the world, by these names.

Afterwards, returning from thence, he thought so highly of himself, on account of the possession of these [magical] arts, as to proclaim himself to be a God. Celsus also adds, That the mother of Jesus became pregnant with him through a soldier, whose name was Panthera[15].

"Was therefore the mother of Jesus beautiful, and was God connected with her on account of her beauty, though he is not adapted to be in love with a corruptible body? Or is it not absurd to suppose that God would be enamoured of a woman who was neither fortunate nor of royal extraction, nor even scarcely known to her neighbours; and who was also hated and ejected by the carpenter her husband, so as neither to be saved by her own credulity nor by divine power? These things, therefore, do not at all pertain to the kingdom of God."

Celsus, again personifying a Jew, says to Christ, "When you were washed by John, you say that the spectre of a bird flew to you from the air. But what witness worthy of belief saw this spectre? Or who heard a voice from heaven, adopting you for a son of God, except yourself, and some one of your associates, who was equally a partaker of your wickedness and punishment?

"Jesus having collected as his associates ten or eleven infamous men, consisting of the most wicked publicans and sailors, fled into different places, obtaining food with difficulty, and in a disgraceful manner."

Again, in the person of a Jew, Celsus says to Christ, "What occasion

---

[15] The same thing is said of Jesus in a work called "The Gospel according to the Jews, or Toldoth Jesu." See Chap. I. and II. of that work.

4

was there, while you were yet an infant, that you should be brought to Egypt, in order that you might not be slain? For it was not fit that a God should be afraid of death. But an angel came from heaven, ordering you and your associates to fly, lest being taken you should be put to death. For the great God [it seems] could not preserve you, his own son, m your own country, but sent two angels on your account."

The same Jew in Celsus also adds, "Though we do not believe in the ancient fables, which ascribe a divine origin to Perseus, Amphion, Æacus, and Minos, yet at the same time their deeds are demonstrated to be mighty and admirable, and truly superhuman, in order that what is narrated of their origin may not appear to be improbable." But (speak-ing to Jesus) he says, "What beautiful or admirable thing have you said or done, though you was (sp) called upon in the temple to give some manifest sign that you were the son of God?"

Celsus, pretending not to disbelieve in the miracles ascribed to Christ, says to him, "Let us grant that these things were performed by you; but they are common with the works of enchanters, who promise to effect more wonderful deeds than these, and also with what those who have been taught by the Egyptians to perform in the middle of the forum for a few oboli; such as expelling dæmons from men, dissipating diseases by a puff, evocating the souls of heroes, exhibiting sumptuous suppers, and tables covered with food, which have no reality. These magicians also represent animals as moving, which are not in reality animals, but merely appear to the imagination to be such.—Is it fit, therefore» that we should believe these men to be the sons of God, because they worked these wonders? Or ought we not rather to say, that these are the arts of depraved and unhappy men!"

5

Again the Jew says, "It is but recently, and as it were yesterday, since we punished Christ; and you, who are [in no respect superior to] keepers of oxen, have abandoned the laws of your ancestors and country. Why likewise do you begin from our sacred institutions, but afterwards in the progress [of your iniquity] despise them? For you have no other origin of your dogma, than our law. Many. other such persons also as Jesus was, may be seen by those who wish to be deceived. How too is it probable that we, who have declared to all men that a person would be sent by God as a punisher of the unjust, should treat him ignominiously, if such a person had appeared among us? Again: How can we think him to be a God, who, that I may omit other things, performed, as we learn, nothing that was promised? And when, being condemned by us, he was thought worthy of punishment, having concealed himself and fled, was most disgracefully made a prisoner; being betrayed by those whom he called his disciples? If, however, he was a God, it was not proper that he should either fly, or be led away captive. And much less was it fit, that, being considered as a saviour and the son of the greatest God, and; also the messenger of this God, by his familiars and private associates, he should be deserted and betrayed by them. But what excellent general, who was the leader of many myriads of men, was ever betrayed by his soldiers? Indeed, this has not happened even to the chief of a band of robbers, though a man depraved, and the captain of men still more depraved than himself, when to his associates he appeared to be useful. But Christ, who was betrayed by those of whom he was the leader, though not as a good commander, nor in such a way as robbers would behave to their captain, could not obtain the benevolence of his deluded followers.—Many other things also, and such as are true, respecting Jesus might be adduced, though they are not committed to writing by his disciples; but these I willingly omit. His disciples also falsely

6

pretended, that he foreknew and foretold every thing that happened to him.

"The disciples of Jesus, not being able to adduce any thing respecting him that was obviously manifest, falsely assert that he foreknew all things; and have written other things of a similar kind respecting lum. This, however, is just the same as if some one should assert that a certain person is a just man, and notwithstanding this should show that he acted unjustly; that he is a pious man, and yet a murderer; and, though immortal, died; at the same time adding to all these assertions, that he had a foreknowledge of all things.

"These things Jesus said after he had previously declared that he was God, and it was entirely necessary that what he had predicted should take place. He therefore, though a God, induced his disciples and prophets, with whom he ate and drank, to become impious. It was, however, requisite that he should have been beneficial to all men, and particularly to his associates. No one likewise would think of betraying the man, of whose table he had been a partaker. But here the associate of the table of God became treacherous to him; God himself, which is still more absurd, making those who had been hospitably entertained by him to be his impious betrayers."

The Jew in Celsus also says, that "What is asserted by the Jewish prophets may be much more probably adapted to ten thousand other persons than to Jesus. Besides, the prophets say, that he who was to come would be a great and powerful king, and would be the lord of the whole earth, and of all nations and armies: but no one would infer from such like symbols and rumours, and from such ignoble arguments, that Christ is the son of God.

7

"As the sun, which illuminates all other things, first shows himself [to be the cause of light], thus also it is fit that this should have been done by the son of God[16]. But the Christians argue sophistically, when they say that the son of God is the word itself. And the accusation is strengthened by this, that the word which was announced by the Christians to be the son of God, was not a pure and holy word, but a man who was most disgracefully punished and put to death.

"What illustrious deed did Jesus accomplish worthy of a God, who beholds from on high with contempt [the trifling pursuits of men, and derides and considers as sport terrestrial events?

"Why too did not Jesus, if not before, yet now at least, [i. e. when he was brought before Pilate,] exhibit some divine indication respecting himself; liberate himself from this ignominy, and punish those who had insulted both him and his father? What kind of ichör also or blood dropped from his crucified body? was it,.....such as from the blest immortals flows?"[17]

The Jew in Celsus further adds: "Do you reproach us with this, O most faithful men, that we do not conceive Christ to be God, and that we do not accord with you in believing that he suffered these things for the benefit of mankind, in order that we also might despise punishment? Neither did he persuade any one while he lived, not even his own disciples, that he should be punished, and suffer as he did: nor did he exhibit himself [though a God] as one liberated from all evils.

---

[16] Celsus means that Christ should have given indubitable evidence, by his sayings, his deeds, and by all that happened to him, that he was the son of God.

[17] See Iliad, V, ver. S40.

8

"Certainly you Christians will not say, that Christ, when he found that he could not induce the inhabitants on the surface of the earth to believe in his doctrines, descended to the infernal regions, in order that he might persuade those that dwelt there. But if inventing absurd apologies by which you are ridiculously deceived, what should hinder others also, who have perished miserably, from being ranked among angels of a more divine order?"

The Jew in Celsus further observes, on comparing Christ with robbers, "Some might in a similar manner unblushingly say of a robber and a homicide, who was punished for his crimes, that he was not a robber but a God; for he predicted to his associates that he should suffer what he did suffer.

"The disciples of Jesus, living with him, hearing his voice, and embracing his doctrines, when they saw that he was punished and put to death, neither died with nor for him, nor could be persuaded to despise punishment; but denied that they were his disciples. Why, therefore, do not you Christians [voluntarily] die with your master?"

The Jew in Celsus also says, that "Jesus made converts of ten sailors, and most abandoned publicans; but did not even persuade all these to embrace his doctrines.

"Is it not also absurd in the extreme, that so many should believe in the doctrines of Christ now he is dead, though he was not able to persuade any one [genuinely] while he was living?

"But the Christians will say, We believe Jesus to be the son of God, because he cured the lame and the blind, and, as you assert, raised the dead.

"O light and truth, which clearly proclaims in its own words, as you write, that other men, and these depraved and enchanters, will come among you, possessing similar miraculous powers! Christ also feigns that a certain being, whom he denominates Satan, will be the source of these nefarious characters: so that Christ himself does not deny that these arts possess nothing divine, and acknowledges that they are the works of depraved men. At the same time likewise, being compelled by truth, he discloses both the arts of others and his own. Is it not, therefore, a miserable thing, to consider, from the performance of the same deeds, this man to be a God, but others to be nothing more than enchanters? For why, employing his testimony, should we rather think those other workers of miracles to be more depraved than himself? Indeed Christ confesses that these arts are not indications of a divine nature, but of certain impostors, and perfectly wicked characters."

After this, the Jew in Celsus says to his fellow-citizens who believed in Jesus, as follows: "Let us grant you that Jesus predicted his resurrection: but how many others have employed such-like prodigies, in order by a fabulous narration to effect what they wished; persuading stupid auditors to believe in these miracles? Zamolxis among the Scythians, who was a slave of Pythagoras, used this artifice; Pythagoras also himself, in Italy; and in Egypt, Rhampsinitus. For it is related of the latter that he played at dice with Ceres in Hades, and that he brought back with him as a gift from her a golden towel. Similar artifices were likewise employed by Orpheus among the Odryssians; by Protesilaus among the Thessalians; and by Hercules and Theseus in Tænarus. This, however, is to be considered,—whether any one who in reality died, ever rose again in the same body: unless you think that the narrations of others are fables,but that your catastrophe of the drama will be found to be either elegant or probable, respecting what was said by him who expired on the cross, and the earthquake, and the darkness, which then according to you ensued. To which may be added, that he who when living could not help himself, arose, as you say, after he was dead, and exhibited the marks of his punishment, and his hands which had been perforated on the cross. But who was it that saw this? A furious woman, as you acknowledge, or some other of the same magical sect; or one who was under the delusion of dreams, and who voluntarily subjected himself to fallacious phantasms, — a thing which happens to myriads of the human race. Or, which is more probable, those who pretended to see this were such as wished to astonish others by this prodigy, and, through a false narration of this kind, to give assistance to the frauds of other impostors.

"Is it to be believed that Christ, when he was alive, openly announced to all men what he was; but when it became requisite that he should procure a strong belief of his resurrection from the dead, he should only show himself secretly to one woman and to his associates?

"If also Christ wished to be concealed, why was a voice heard from heaven, proclaiming him to be the son of God? Or, if he did not wish to be concealed, why did he suffer punishment, and why did, he [ignominiously] die?"

The Jew in Celsus likewise adds, "These things therefore we have adduced to you from your own writings, than which we have employed no other testimony, for you yourselves are by them confuted. Besides, what God that ever appeared to men, did not procure belief that he was a God, particularly when he appeared to those who expected his advent? Or why was he not acknowledged by those, by whom he had been for a long time expected? We certainly hope for a resurrection in the body, and that we shall have eternal life. We also believe that the paradigm and primary leader of this, will be he who is to be sent to us; and who will show that it is not impossible for God to raise any one with his body that he pleases."

After this, Celsus in his own person says, "The Christians and Jews most stupidly contend with each other, and this controversy of theirs about Christ differs in nothing from the proverb about the contention for the shadow of an ass[18]. There is also nothing venerable in the investigation of the Jews and Christians with each other; both of them believing that there was a certain prophecy from a divine spirit, that a saviour of the human race would appear on the earth, but disagreeing in their opinion whether he who was predicted had appeared or not.

"The Jews originating from the Egyptians deserted Egypt through sedition, at the same time despising the religion of the Egyptians. Hence the same thing happened to the Christians afterwards, who abandoned the religion of the Jews, as to the Jews who revolted from the Egyptians; for the cause to both of their innovation was a seditious opposition to the common[19] and established rites of their country.

"The Christians at first, when they were few, had but one opinion;

---

[18] This proverb is mentioned by Apuleius at the end of the Ninth Book of his Metamorphosis. There is also another Greek proverb mentioned by Menander, Plato, and many others, [−Greek−], concerning the shadow of an ass, which is said of those who are anxious to know things futile, frivolous, and entirely useless. These two proverbs Apuleius has merged into one.

[19] In the original [−Greek−], but it is necessary to read, conformably to the above translation, [−Greek−]

but when they became scattered through their multitude, they were again and again divided into sects, and each sect wished to have an establishment of its own. For this was what they desired to effect from the beginning.

"But after they were widely dispersed one sect opposed the other, nor did any thing remain common to them except the name of Christians; and even this they were at the same time ashamed to leave as a common appellation: but as to other things, they were the ordinances of men of a different persuasion.

"What however is still more wonderful is this, that their doctrine may be [easily] confuted, as consisting of no hypothesis worthy of belief. But their dissension among themselves, the advantage they derive from it, and their dread of those who are not of their belief, give stability to their faith.

"The Christians ridicule the Egyptians, though they indicated many and by no means contemptible things through enigmas, when they taught that honours should be paid to eternal ideas, and not, as it appears to the vulgar, to diurnal animals[20]." Celsus adds, that "The Christians stupidly introduce nothing more venerable than the goats and dogs of the Egyptians in their narrations respecting Jesus.

"What is said by a few who are considered as Christians, concerning the doctrine of Jesus and the precepts of Christianity, is not designed for the wiser, but for the more unlearned and ignorant part of mankind. For the following are their precepts: 'Let no one who is erudite accede to us, no one who is wise, no one who is prudent (for these things are thought by us to be evil); but let any one who is unlearned, who is stupid, who is an infant in

---

[20] See on this subject the Treatise of Plutarch respecting Isis and Osiris.

13

understanding boldly come to us.' For the Christians openly acknowledge that such as these are worthy to be noticed by their God; manifesting by this, that they alone wish and are able to persuade the ignoble, the insensate, slaves, stupid women, and little children and fools.

"We may see in the forum infamous characters and jugglers[21] collected together, who dare not show their tricks to intelligent men; but when they perceive a lad, and a crowd of slaves and stupid men, they endeavour to ingratiate themselves with such characters as these.

"We also may see in their own houses, wool-weavers, shoemakers, fullers, and the most illiterate and rustic men, who dare not say any thing in the presence of more elderly and wiser fathers of families; but when they meet with children apart from their parents, and certain stupid women with them, then they discuss something of a wonderful nature; such as that it is not proper to pay attention to parents and preceptors, but that they should be persuaded by them. For, say they, your parents and preceptors are delirious and stupid, and neither know what is truly good, nor are able to effect it, being prepossessed with trifles of an unusual nature. They add, that they alone know how it is proper to live, and that if children are persuaded by them, they will be blessed, and also the family to which they belong. At the same time likewise that they say this, if they see any one of the wiser teachers of erudition approaching, or the father of the child to whom they are speaking, such of them as are more cautious defer their discussion to another time; but those that are more audacious, urge the children to shake off the reins of

---

[21] Celsus, as we are informed by Origen, compares the Christians with men of this description.

14

parental authority, whispering to them, that when their fathers and preceptors are present, they neither wish nor are able to unfold to children what is good, as they are deterred by the folly and rusticity of these men, who are entirely corrupted, are excessively depraved, and would punish them [their true admonishers]. They further add, that if they wish to be instructed by them, it is requisite that they should leave their parents and preceptors, and go with women and little children, who are their playfellows, to the conclave of women, or to the shoemaker's or fuller's shop, that they may obtain perfection [by embracing their doctrines].

"That I do not however accuse the Christians more bitterly than truth compels, may be conjectured from hence, that the criers who call men to other mysteries proclaim as follows: 'Let him approach, whose hands are pure, and whose words are wise.' And again, others proclaim: 'Let him approach, who is pure from all wickedness, whose soul is not conscious of any evil, and who leads a just and upright life.' And these things are proclaimed by those who promise a purification from error. Let us now hear who those are that are called to the Christian mysteries. 'Whoever is a sinner, whoever is unwise, whoever is a fool, and whoever, in short, is miserable, him the kingdom of God will receive.' Do you not therefore call a sinner, an unjust man, a thief, a housebreaker, a wizard, one who is sacrilegious, and a robber of sepulchres? What other persons would the crier nominate, who should call robbers together?

"God, according to the Christians, descended to men; and, as consequent to this, it was fancied that he had left his own proper abode.

"God, however, being unknown among men [as the Christians say],

15

and in consequence of this appearing to be in a condition inferior to that of a divine being, was not willing to be known, and therefore made trial of those who believed and of those who did not believe in him; just as men who have become recently rich, call on God as a witness of their abundant and entirely mortal ambition.

"The Christians have asserted nothing paradoxical or new concerning a deluge or a conflagration, but have perverted the doctrine of the Greeks and barbarians, that in long periods of time, and recursions and concursions of the stars, conflagrations and deluges take place; and also that after the last deluge, which was that of Deucalion, the period required, conformably to the mutation of wholes, a conflagration[22]. This the Christians, however, have perverted by representing God as descending with fire as a spy.

"Again, we will repeat and confirm by many arguments, an assertion which has nothing in it novel, but was formerly universally acknowledged. God is good, is beautiful and blessed, and his very nature consists in that which is most beautiful and the best. If therefore he descended to men, his nature must necessarily be changed. But the change must be from good to evil, and from the beautiful to the base, from felicity to infelicity, and from that which is most excellent to that which is most worthless. Who, however, would choose to be thus changed? Besides, to be changed and transformed pertains to that which is naturally mortal; but an invariable sameness of subsistence is the prerogative of an immortal nature. Hence God could never receive a mutation of this kind[23].

---

[22] See Taylor's translation of Proclus on the Timæus of Plato, Book I.
[23] See a most admirable defence of the immutability of Divinity, by Proclus, in Taylor's Introduction to the Second and Third Books of Plato's

"Either God is in reality changed, as the Christians say, into a mortal body,—and we have before shown that this is impossible; or he himself is not changed, but he causes those who behold him to think that he is, and thus falsifies himself, and involves others in error. Deception, however, and falsehood are indeed otherwise evil, and can only be [properly] employed by any one as a medicine, either in curing friends that are diseased or have some vicious propensity, or those that are insane, or for the purpose of avoiding danger from enemies. But no one who has vicious propensities, or is insane, is dear to Divinity. Nor does God fear any one, in order that by wandering he may escape danger[24].

"The Christians, adding to the assertions of the Jews, say that the son of God came on account of the sins of the Jews; and that the Jews, punishing Jesus and causing him to drink gall, raised the bile of God against them."

Celsus after this, in his usual way deriding both Jews and Christians, compares all of them to a multitude of bats, or to ants coming out of their holes, or to frogs seated about a marsh, or to earthworms that assemble in a corner of some muddy place, and contend with each other which of them are most noxious. He likewise represents them as saying, "God has manifested and predicted all things to us; and deserting the whole world and the celestial circulation, and likewise paying no attention to the widely-extended earth, he regards our concerns alone, to us alone sends messengers, and he will never cease to explore by what means we

---

Republic, in vol. i. of his translation of Plato's Works. See also Taylor's note at the end of vol. iii. of his translation of Pausanias, p. 235.
[24] The original of this sentence is, [—Greek—] the latter part of which, [—Greek—], is thus, erroneously translated by Spencer, "ut imposture opus habeat ad evadendum periculum."

17

may always associate with him." He likewise resembles us to earthworms acknowledging that God exists; and he says that we earthworms, i. e. the Jews and Christians, being produced by God after him, are entirely similar to him. All things too are subject to us, earth and water, the air and the stars, and are ordained to be subservient to us[25]. Afterwards these earthworms add: "Now because some of us have sinned, God will come, or he will send his son, in order that he may burn the unjust, and that those who are not so may live eternally with him." And Celsus concludes with observing that "such assertions would be more tolerable if they were made by earthworms or frogs, than by Jews or Christians contending with each other."

Celsus, after having adduced, from the writings of the heathens, instances of those who contended for the antiquity of their race, such as the Athenians, Egyptians, Arcadians, and Phrygians, and also of those who have asserted that some among them were aborigines, says, that "the Jews being concealed in a corner of Palestine, men perfectly in-erudite, and who never had previously heard the same things celebrated by Hesiod and innumerable other divine men, composed a most incredible and inelegant narration, that a certain man was fashioned by the hands of God, and inspired

---

[25] This reminds me of the following beautiful lines in Epistle I. of Pope's Essay on Man, in which Pride is represented as saying:

"For me kind nature wakes her genial power,
Suckles each herb, and spreads out every flower;
Annual for me the grape, the rose, renew
The juice nectarious and the balmy dew.
For me the mine a thousand treasures brings:
For me health gushes from a thousand springs;
Seas roll to waft me, suns to light me rise,
My footstool earth, my canopy the skies."

by him with the breath of life; that a woman was taken from the side of the man; that precepts were given to them by God; and that a serpent was adverse to these precepts. Lastly, they make the serpent to frustrate the commands of God: in all this, narrating a certain fable worthy only of being told by old women, and which most impiously makes God to be from the first imbecile, and incapable of persuading one man fashioned by himself to act in a way conformable to his will.

"The Christians are most impiously deceived and involved in error, through the greatest ignorance of the meaning of divine enigmas. For they make a certain being whom they call the Devil, and who in the Hebrew tongue is denominated Satan, hostile to God. It is therefore perfectly stupid and unholy to assert that the greatest God, wishing to benefit mankind, was incapable of accomplishing what he wished, through having one that opposed him, and acted contrary to his will. The son of God, therefore, was vanquished by the devil; and being punished by him, teaches us also to despise the punishments inflicted by him; Christ at the same time predicting that Satan would appear on the earth, and, like himself, would exhibit great and admirable works, usurping to himself the glory of God. The son of God also adds, that it is not fit to pay attention to Satan, because he is a seducer, but that himself alone is worthy of belief. This, however, is evidently the language of a man who is an impostor earnestly endeavouring to prevent, and previously guarding himself against, the attempts of those who think differently from and oppose him. But, according to the Christians, the son of God is punished by the devil, who also punishes us in order that through this we may be exercised in endurance. These assertions, however, are perfectly ridiculous. For it is fit, I think, that the devil should be punished, and not that men should be threatened with punishment who are calumniated by him.

19

"Further still: If God, like Jupiter in the comedy, being roused from a long sleep, wished to liberate the human race from evils, why did he send only into a corner of the earth this spirit of whom you boast? though he ought in a similar manner to have animated many other bodies, and to have sent them to every part of the habitable globe. The comic poet indeed, in order to excite the laughter of the audience in the theatre, says that Jupiter, after he was roused from his sleep, sent Mercury to the Athenians and Lacedæmonsians:— but do not you think that it is a much more ridiculous fiction to assert that God sent his son to the Jews?

"Many—and these, men whose names are not known,—both in temples and out of temples, and some also assembling in cities or armies, are easily excited from any casual cause, as if they possessed a prophetic power. Each of these likewise is readily accustomed to say, 'I am God, or the son of God, or a divine spirit. But I came because the world will soon be destroyed, and you, O men! on account of your iniquities will perish. I wish, however, to save you, and you shall again see me, returning with a celestial army. Blessed is he who now worships me; but I will cast all those who do not, into eternal fire, together with the cities and regions to which they belong. Those men also that do not now know the punishments which are reserved for them, shall afterwards repent and lament in vain: but those who believe in me I will for ever save.' Extending to the multitude these insane and perfectly obscure assertions, the meaning of which no intelligent man is able to discover,—for they are unintelligible and a mere nothing,—they afford an occasion to the stupid and to jugglers of giving to them whatever interpretation they please.

"Again, they do not consider, if the prophets of the God of the Jews had predicted that this would be his son, why did this God legislatively ordain through Moses, that the Jews should enrich themselves and acquire power; should fill the earth with their progeny; and should slay and cut off the whole race of their enemies, which Moses did, as he says, in the sight of the Jews; and besides this, threatening that unless they were obedient to these his commands, he should consider them as his enemies;—why, after these things had been promulgated by God, did his son, a Nazarean man, exclude from any access to his father, the rich and powerful, the wise and renowned? For he says that we ought to pay no more attention than ravens do, to food and the necessaries of life[26], and that we should be less concerned about our clothing than the lilies of the field. Again, he asserts, that to him who smites us on one cheek we should likewise turn the other[27]. Whether, therefore, does Moses or Jesus lie? Or, was the Father who sent Jesus forgetful of what he had formerly said to Moses? Or, condemning his own laws, did he alter his opinion, and send a messenger to mankind with mandates of a contrary nature?

"The Christians again will say, How can God be known unless he can be apprehended by sense? To this we reply, that such a question is not the interrogation of man, nor of soul, but of the flesh. At the same time, therefore, let them hear, if they are capable of hearing any thing, as being a miserable worthless race, and lovers of body! If, closing the perceptive organs of sense, you look upward with the visive power of intellect, and, averting the eye of the flesh, you excite the eye of the soul, you will thus alone behold God[28]. And if you seek for the leader of this path, you must avoid impostors and enchanters, and those who persuade you to pay

---

[26] Luke xii. 24.

[27] Luke vi. 29.

[28] This is most Platonically said by Celsus.

21

attention to [real] idols; in order that you may not be entirely ridiculous, by blaspheming as idols other things which are manifestly Gods[29], and venerating that which is in reality more worthless than any image, and which is not even an image, but a dead body[30]; and by investigating a Father similar to it.

"There are essence and generation, the intelligible and the visible. And truth indeed subsists with essence, but error with generation[31]. Science, therefore, is conversant with truth, but opinion with generation. Intelligence also pertains to, or has the intelligible for its object; but what is visible is the object of sight. And intellect indeed knows the intelligible; but the eye knows that which is visible. What the sun therefore is in the visible region,—being neither the eye, nor sight, but the cause to the eye of seeing, and to the sight of its visive power, to all sensibles of their being generated, and to himself of being perceived;—this the supreme God [or the good] is

---

[29] Such as the sun and moon, and the other heavenly bodies.

[30] The Emperor Julian in the fragments of his Arguments against the Christians, 'preserved by Cyril, says, speaking to the Christians: "You do not notice whether any thing is said by the Jews about holiness; but you emulate their rage and their bitterness, overturning temples and altars, and cutting the throats not only of those who remain firm in paternal institutes, but also of those heretics who are equally erroneous with yourselves, and who do not lament a dead body in the same manner as you do. For neither Jesus nor Paul exhorted you to act in this manner. But the reason is, that they did not expect you would arrive at the power which you have obtained. For they were satisfied if they could deceive maid-servants and slaves, and through these married women, and such men as Cornelius and Sergius; among whom, if you can mention one that was at that time an illustrious character, (and these things were transacted under the reign of Tiberius or Claudius,) believe that I am a liar in all things."

[31] Generation signifies the whole of that which is visible.

in intelligibles: since he is neither intellect, nor intelligence, nor science, but is the cause, to intellect, of intellectual perception; to intelligence, of its subsistence on account of him; to science, for its possession of knowledge for his sake, and to all intelligibles for their existence as such. He is likewise the cause to truth itself and to essence itself, of their existence, being himself beyond all intelligibles, by a certain ineffable power[32]. And these are the assertions of men who possess intellect. But if you understand any thing of what is here said, you are indebted to us for it. If, likewise, you think that a certain spirit descending from God announced to you things of a divine nature, this will be the spirit which proclaimed what I have above said, and with which ancient men being replete, have unfolded so many things of a most beneficial nature. If, therefore, you are unable to understand these assertions, be silent, and conceal your ignorance, and do not say that those are blind who see, and that those are lame who run, you at the same time possessing souls that are in every respect lame and mutilated, and living in body, viz. in that which is dead.

"How much better would it be for you, since you are desirous of innovation, to direct your attention to some one of the illustrious dead, and concerning whom a divine fable may be properly admitted! And if Hercules and Esculapius do not please you, and other renowned men of great antiquity, you may have Orpheus, a man confessedly inspired by a sacred spirit, and who suffered a

---

[32] This sentence in the original is as follows: [—Greek—]. But it is requisite to read, conformably to the above translation, [—Greek—]. Celsus has derived what he here says from the Sixth Book of Plato's Republic, and what he says previous to this from the Timæus of Plato.—See Taylor's translation of these Dialogues.

violent death. But he perhaps has been adopted as a leader formerly by others. Consider Anaxarchus, therefore, who being thrown into a mortar, and bruised in the cruellest manner, most courageously despised the punishment, exclaiming, 'Bruise, bruise the sack of Anaxarchus, for you cannot bruise him.' This, indeed, was uttered by a certain truly divine spirit. Him, however, some physiologists have already vindicated to themselves. In the next place, consider Epictetus, who when his master twisted his leg violently, said, smiling gently and without being terrified, 'You will break my leg;' and when his master had broken his leg, only observed, 'Did I not tell you that you would break it? What thing of this kind did your God utter when he was punished[33]? The sibyl, likewise, whose verses are used by some of you, is far more worthy to be regarded by you as the daughter of God. But now you have fraudulently and rashly inserted in her verses many things of a blasphemous nature[34]; and Christ, who in his life was most reprehensible, and in his death most miserable, you reverence as a God. How much more appropriately might you have bestowed this honour on Jonas when he was under the gourd, or on Daniel who was saved in the den of lions, or on others of whom more prodigious things than these are narrated!

"This is one of the precepts of the Christians: 'Do not revenge yourself on him who injures you; and if any person strikes you on

---

[33] Christ when on the cross exclaimed, "My God, my God, why hast thou forsaken me?" But Socrates in his Apology to his Judges, as recorded by Plato, most magnanimously said, "Anytus and Melitus may indeed put me to death, but they cannot injure me."

[34] The collection of the Sibylline Oracles which are now extant, are acknowledged by all intelligent men among the learned to be for the most part forgeries.—See the account of them by Fabricius in vol. i. of his Bibliootheca Græca.

one cheek, turn the other to him also.' And this precept indeed is of very great antiquity, but is recorded in a more rustic manner by Christ. For Socrates is made by Plata in the Crito to speak as follows: 'It is by no means therefore proper to do an injury. By no means. Hence neither is it proper for him who is injured to revenge the injury, as the multitude think it is; since it is by no means fit to do an injury. It does not appear that it is. But what! is it proper or not, O Crito, to be malific? It certainly is not proper, Socrates. Is it therefore just or unjust for a man to be malific to him by whom he has been hurt? for in the opinion of the vulgar it is just. It is by no means just. For to be hurtful to men does not at all differ from injuring them. You speak the truth. Neither, therefore, is it proper to revenge an injury, nor to be hurtful to any man, whatever evil we may suffer from him.' These things are asserted by Plato, who also adds: 'Consider, therefore, well, whether you agree, and are of the same opinion with me in this; and we will begin with admitting, that it is never right either to do an injury, or revenge an injury on him who has acted badly towards us. Do you assent to this principle? For formerly it appeared, and now still appears, to me to be true.' Such, therefore, was the opinion of Plato, and which also was the doctrine of divine men prior to him. Concerning these, however, and other particulars which the Christians have corrupted, enough has been said. For he who desires to search further into them, may easily be satisfied.

"But why is it requisite to enumerate how many things have been foretold with a divinely inspired voice, partly by prophetesses and prophets, and partly by other men and women under the influence of inspiration? What wonderful things they have heard from the adyta themselves! How many things have been rendered manifest from victims and sacrifices to those who have used them! How

25

many from other prodigious symbols! And to some persons, divinely luminous appearances have been manifestly present. Of these things indeed the life of every one is full. How many cities, likewise, have been raised from oracles, and liberated from disease and pestilence! And how many, neglecting these, or forgetting them, have perished miserably! How many colonies have been founded from these, and by observing their mandates have been rendered happy! How many potentates and private persons have, from attending to or neglecting these, obtained a better or a worse condition! How many, lamenting their want of children, have through these obtained the object of their wishes! How many have escaped the anger of dæmons! How many mutilated bodies have been healed! And again, how many have immediately suffered for insolent behaviour in sacred concerns! some indeed becoming insane on the very spot; others proclaiming their impious deeds, but others not proclaiming them before they perished; some destroying themselves, and others becoming a prey to incurable diseases. And sometimes a dreadful voice issuing from the adyta has destroyed them[35].

"In the next place, is it not absurd that you should desire and hope for the resurrection of the body, as if nothing was more excellent or more honourable to us than this; and yet again, that you should hurl this same body into punishments, as a thing of a vile nature? To men, however, who are persuaded that this is true, and who are conglutinated to body, it is not worth while to speak of things of this kind. For these are men who in other respects are rustic and impure, without reason, and labouring under the disease of sedition. Indeed, those who hope that the soul or intellect will exist

---

[35] See the scientific theory of Oracles unfolded in the Notes to Taylor's translation of Pausanias, vol. iii. p. 259.

eternally, whether they are willing to call it pneumatic[36], or an intellectual spirit holy and blessed, or a living soul, or the supercelestial and incorruptible progeny of a divine and incorporeal nature[37], or whatever other appellation they may think fit to give it; those who thus hope, (but I say this in accordance with Divinity,) in this respect think rightly, that those who have lived well in this life will be blessed, but that those who have been entirely unjust, will be involved in endless evils. And neither the Christians nor any other man were ever hostile to this dogma.

"Since men are bound to body, whether they are so for the sake of the dispensation of the whole of things, or in order that they may suffer the punishment of their offences, or in consequence of the soul through certain passions becoming heavy and tending downwards, till through certain orderly periods it becomes purified;—for according to Empedocles, it is necessary that.

From the blest wandering thrice ten thousand[38] times, Through various mortal forms the soul should pass.'— This being the case, it is requisite to believe that men are committed to the care of certain inspective guardians of this prison the body.

"That to the least of things, however, are allotted guardian powers, may be learnt from the Egyptians, who say that the human body is

---

[36] This is said conformably to the opinion of the Stoics.

[37] This is asserted in accordance with the doctrine of the Platonists.

[38] This 30,000 times must not be considered mathematically; since it symbolically indicates a certain appropriate measure of perfection. For in units S is a perfect number, as having a beginning, middle, and end. And again, 10 is perfect, because it comprehends all numbers in itself. These numbers, however, were called by the ancients perfect, in a different way from 6, 28, &c.; for these were thus denominated because they are equal to the sum of their parts.

27

divided into thirty-six parts, and that dæmons[39] or certain etherial gods who are distributed into the same number of parts, are the guardians of these divisions of the body. Some also assert, that there is a much greater number of these presiding powers; different corporeal parts being under the inspection of different powers. The names of these also in the vernacular tongue of the Egyptians are Chnoumën, Chnachoumën, Knat, Sicat, Biou, Erou, Erebiou, Ramanor, Reianoor. What, therefore, should prevent him from making use of these and other powers, who wishes rather to be well than to be ill, to be fortunate rather than to be unfortunate, and to be liberated from such tormentors and castigators as these things are thought to be?[40]

"He, however, who invokes these powers ought to be careful, lest being conglutinated [as it were] to the worship of them, and to a love of the body, he should turn from and become oblivious of more excellent natures. For it is perhaps requisite not to disbelieve in wise men, who say that the greater part of circumterrestrial dæmons are conglutinated to generation, and are delighted with blood, with the odour and vapour of flesh, with melodies and with other things of the like kind[41]; to which being bound, they are unable to effect any thing superior to the sanction of the body, and the prediction of future events to men and cities. Whatever also pertains to mortal actions they know, and are able to bring to pass.

---

[39] i. e. beneficent dæmonss; for the ancients divided dæmonss into the beneficent and malevolent. They also considered the former as assisting the soul in its ascent to its pristine state of felicity; but the latter as of a punishing and avenging characteristic.

[40] Vid. Salmas. In fine libri He Annis climactericis.

[41] See Book II. of Taylor's translation of Porphyry,—On Abstinence from Animal Food.

"If some one should command a worshiper of God either to act impiously, or to say any thing of a most disgraceful nature, he is in no respect whatever to be obeyed; but all trial and every kind of death are to be endured rather than to meditate, and much more to assert, any thing impious concerning God. But if any one should order us to celebrate the Sun or Minerva, we ought most gladly to sing hymns to their praise. For thus you will appear to venerate the supreme God in a greater degree[42], if you also celebrate these powers: for piety when it passes through all things becomes more perfect."

---

[42] For as the ineffable principle of things possesses all power and the highest power, he first produced from himself beings most transcendently allied to himself; and therefore, by venerating these, the highest God will be in a greater degree venerated, as being a greater veneration of his power.

# EXTRACTS FROM, AND INFORMATION RELATIVE TO, THE TREATISE OF PORPHYRY

This work of Porphyry consisted of Fifteen Books, and is unfortunately lost. It is frequently mentioned by the Fathers of the Church, from whose writings the following particulars are collected.

The First Book appears to have contained a development of the contrariety of the Scriptures, and proofs that they did not proceed from Divinity, but from men. To this end Porphyry especially adduces what Paul writes to the Galatians, chap. ii. viz. that "when Peter came to Antioch, he withstood him to his face, because he was to be blamed." Hence Porphyry infers, "that the Apostles, and indeed the chief of them, did not publicly study the salvation of all men, but that each of them was privately attentive to his own renown." This the Fathers testify in more than one place. See the Commentary of Jerome on the above-mentioned Epistle. Jerome also, in his 89th Epistle to Augustin, informs us that Porphyry says, "that Peter and Paul opposed each other in a puerile contest, and that Paul was envious of the virtue of Peter."

The Third Book treated of the interpretation of the Scriptures, in which Porphyry condemned the mode of explaining them adopted by the commentators, and especially the allegories of Origen. This is evident from a long extract from this work of Porphyry given by Eusebius in Hist. Eccl. lib. i. cap. 13.

The Fourth Book treated of the Mosaic history and the antiquities of the Jews, as we learn from Eusebius, Proep. Evang. lib. i. cap. 9, and from Theo-doret, Serm. ii. Therap.

But the Twelfth Book was the most celebrated of all, in which Porphyry strenuously opposes the prophecy of Daniel. Of this work Jerome thus speaks in the Preface to his Commentary on that prophet: "Porphyry's twelfth book is against the prophet Daniel, as he was unwilling to admit that it was written by that prophet, but contends that it was composed by a person in Judæa named Epiphanes, and who lived in the time of Antiochus. Hence he says, that Daniel does not so much narrate future as past events. Lastly, he asserts, that whatever is related as far as to the reign of Antiochus contains a true history; but that all that is said posterior to this time, as the writer was ignorant of futurity, is false."

The Thirteenth Book also, according to Jerome[43], was written against the same prophet; in which book, speaking of the "abomination of desolation," as it is called by Daniel, (when standing in the sacred place,) he says many reproachful things of the Christians.

The same Jerome likewise, in Epist. ci., ad Pam-machium, testifies, that Porphyry accuses the history of the Evangelists of falsehood,

---

[43] Vid. lib. iv. Comment, in 24 Cap. Matth.

and says[44] that Christ, after he had told his brethren that he should not go up to the feast of tabernacles, yet afterwards went up to it (John vii.). Hence Porphyry accuses him of inconstancy and mutability. Jerome's observation on this is curious, viz. "Nesciens omnia scandala ad carnem esse referenda."

Jerome adds (in Lib. Quasst. Hebraic, in Genesin) "that Porphyry calumniates the Evangelists for making a miracle to the ignorant, by asserting that Christ walked on the sea, calling the lake Genezareth the sea." He likewise says, that Porphyry called the miracles which were performed at the sepulchres of the martyrs, "the delusions of evil demons."

The following remarkable passage from one of the lost writings of Porphyry relative to the Christians, is preserved by Augustin in his Treatise De Civit. lib. xix. cap. 23.

"Sunt spiritus terreni minimi loco terreno quodam malorum dæmonum potestati subjecti. Ab his sapientes Hebræorum, quorum unus iste etiam Jesus fuit, sicut audivisti divina Apollonis oracula quæ superius dicta sunt. Ab his ergo Hebæi dsemonibus pessimis et minoribus spiritibus vetabant religiosos, et ipsis vacare prohibebant: venerari autem magis coelestes Deos, amplius autem venerari Deum patrem. Hoc autem et Dii præcipiunt, et in superioibus ostendimus, quemadmodum animadvertere ad Deum monent, et ilium colère ubique imperant. Verum indocti et impiæ naturae, quibus vere Fatum non concessit a Dius dona obtinere, neque habere Jovis immortalis notitiam, non audientes Deos et divinos viros; Deos quidem omnes recusaverunt, prohibitos autem dæmones non solum nullis odiis insequi, sed etiam revereri

---

[44] Lib. ii. adversus Pelagianos.

delegerunt. Deum autem simulantes se colère, ea sola per quae Deus adoratur, non agunt. Nam Deus quidem utpote omnium pater nullius indiget: sed nobis est bene, cum eum per justitiam et castitatem, aliasque virtutes adoramus, ipsam vitam precem ad ipsum fa-cientes, per imitationem et inquisitionem de ipso. Inquisitio enim purgat, imitatio deificat affectionem ad ipsum operando."

i. e. "There are terrene spirits of the lowest order, who in a certain terrene place are subject to the power of evil demons. From these were derived the wise men of the Hebrews, of whom Jesus also was one; as you have heard the divine oracles of Apollo above mentioned assert. From these worst of demons therefore, and lesser spirits of the Hebrew, the oracles forbid the religious, and prohibit from paying attention to them, but exhort them rather to venerate the celestial gods, and still more the father of the gods. And we have above shown how the gods admonish us to look to Divinity, and everywhere command us to worship him. But the unlearned and impious natures, to whom Fate has not granted truly to obtain gifts from the gods, and to have a knowledge of immortal Jupiter, — these not attending to the gods and divine men, reject indeed all the gods, and are so far from hating prohibited demons, that they even choose to reverence them[45]. But pretending that they worship God,

---

[45] The Platonic philosopher Sallust, in his golden book On the Gods and the World, says, alluding to the Christians, cap. 18, "Impiety, which invades some places of the earth, and which will often subsist in future, ought not to give any disturbance to the worthy mind; for things of this kind do not affect, nor can religious honours be of any advantage to the gods; and the soul from its middle nature is not always able to pursue that which is right Besides, it is not improbable that impiety is a species of punishment; for those who have known and at the same time despised the gods, we may reasonably suppose will in another life be deprived of the

they do not perform those things through which alone God is adored. For God, indeed, as being the father of all things, is not in want of any thing; but it is well with us when we adore him through justice and continence, and the other virtues, making our life a prayer to him through the imitation and investigation of him. For investigation purifies, but imitation deifies the affection of the mind by energizing about divinity."

The following extract from Porphyry concerning a pestilence which raged for many years at Rome, and could not be mitigated by any sacrifices, is preserved by Theodoret: "[—Greek—]." i. e. "The Christians now wonder that the city has been for so many years attacked by disease, the advent [or manifest appearance] of Esculapius and the other gods no longer existing. For Jesus being now reverenced and worshiped, no one any longer derives any public benefit from the gods."

---

knowledge of their nature. And those who have honoured their proper sovereigns as gods, shall be cut off from the divinities, as the punishment of their impiety."

# A FRAGMENT OF THE THIRTY-FOURTH
# BOOK OF DIODORUS SICULUS

"King Antiochus besieged Jerusalem; but the Jews resisted him for some time. When, however, all their provision was spent, they were forced to send ambassadors to him to treat on terms. Many of his friends persuaded him to storm the city, and

to root out the whole nation of the Jews; because they only, of all people, hated to converse with any of another nation, and treated all of them as enemies. They likewise suggested to him, that the ancestors of the Jews were driven out of Egypt as impious and hateful to the Gods. For their bodies being overspread and infected with the itch and leprosy, they brought them together into one place by way of expiation, and as profane and wicked wretches expelled them from their coasts. Those too that were thus expelled seated themselves about Jerusalem, and being afterwards embodied into one nation, called the nation of the Jews, their hatred of all other men descended with their blood to posterity. Hence they made strange laws, entirely different from those of other nations. In consequence of this, they will neither eat nor drink with any one of a different nation, nor wish him any prosperity. For, say they,

Antiochus, surnamed Epiphanes, having subdued the Jews, entered into the temple of God, into which by their law no one was permitted to enter but the priest. Here, when he found the image of a man with a long beard carved in stone sitting on an ass, he conceived it to be Moses who built Jerusalem, established the nation, and made all their impious customs and practises legal: for these abound in hatred and enmity to all other men. Antiochus, therefore, abhorring this their contrariety to all other nations, used his utmost endeavour to abrogate their laws. In order to effect this, he sacrificed a large hog at the image of Moses and at the altar of God that stood in the outward court, and sprinkled them with the blood of the sacrifice. He commanded likewise that the sacred books, whereby they were taught to hate all other nations, should be sprinkled with the broth made of the hog's flesh. And he extinguished the lamp called by them immortal, which was continually burning in the temple. Lastly, he compelled the high priest and the other Jews to eat swine's flesh. Afterwards, when Antiochus and his friends had deliberately considered these things, they urged him to root out the whole nation, or at least to abrogate their laws and compel them to change their former mode of conducting themselves in common life. But the king being generous and of a mild disposition, received hostages and pardoned the Jews. He demolished, however, the walls of Jerusalem, and took the tribute that was due."

# FROM MANETHO RESPECTING THE ISRAELITES

"While such was the state of things in Ethiopia, the people of Jerusalem, having come down with the defiled of the Egyptians, treated the inhabitants in such an unholy manner, that those who witnessed their impieties, believed that their joint sway was more execrable than that which the shepherds had formerly exercised. For they not only set fire to the cities and villages, but committed every kind of sacrilege, and destroyed the images of the gods, and roasted and fed upon those sacred animals that were worshipped; and having compelled the priests and prophets to kill and sacrifice them, they cast them naked out of the country. It is said also that the priest who ordained their polity and laws was by birth of Heliopolis, and his name Osarsiph, from Osons the god of Heliopolis; but that when he went over to these people, his name was changed, and he was called Moÿses."

Manetho again says: "After this, Amenophis returned from Ethiopia with a great force, and Rampses also his son with other forces; and encountering the shepherds and defiled people, they defeated and slew multitudes of them, add pursued them to the bounds of Syria."—Joseph contn App. lib. i. cap. 26, & 27.

"Cherilus also, a still more ancient writer [than Herodotus], and a poet, makes mention of our nation, and informs us that it came to the assistance of king Xerxes in his expedition against Greece. For in his enumeration of all those nations, he last of all inserts ours among the rest, when he says: "At the last, there passed over a people wonderful to behold; for they spake the Phoenician tongue, and dwelt in the Solymæan mountains, near a broad lake. Their heads were sooty; they had round rasures on them; their heads and faces were like nasty horse heads, also, that had been hardened in the smoke."—Whiston's Josephus, vol. iv. p. 299.

# EXTRACTS FROM THE FIFTH BOOK OF TACITUS RESPECTING THE JEWS, AS

*TRANSLATED BY MURPHY*

"Being now to relate the progress of a siege that terminated in the destruction of that once celebrated city [Jerusalem], it may be proper to go back to its first foundation, and to trace the origin of the people. The Jews we are told were natives of the Isle of Crete. At the time when Saturn was driven from his throne by the violence of Jupiter, they abandoned their habitations, and gained a settlement at the extremity of Libya. In support of this tradition, the etymology of their name is adduced as a proof. Mount Ida, well known to fame, stands in the Isle of Crete: the inhabitants are called Idæans; and the word by a barbarous corruption was changed afterwards to that of Judæans. According to others they were a colony from Egypt, when that country, during the reign of Isis,

overflowing with inhabitants poured forth its redundant numbers under the conduct of Hierosolymus and Juda. A third hypothesis makes them originally Ethiopians, compelled by the tyranny of Cepheus, the reigning monarch, to abandon their country. Some authors contend that they were a tribe of Assyrians, who for some time occupied a portion of Egypt, and afterwards transplanting themselves into Syria, acquired in their own right a number of cities, together with the territories of the Hebrews. There is still another tradition, which ascribes to the Jews a more illustrious origin, deriving them from the ancient Solymans, so highly celebrated in the poetry of Homer. By that people the city was built, and from its founder received the name of Hierosolyma.

"In this clash of opinions, one point seems to be universally admitted. A pestilential disease, disfiguring the race of man, and making the body an object of loathsome deformity, spread all over Egypt. Bocchoris, at that time the reigning monarch, consulted the oracle of Jupiter Ammon, and received for answer that the kingdom must be purified by exterminating the infected multitude as a race of men detested by the gods. After diligent search, the wretched sufferers were collected together, and in a wild and barren desert abandoned to their misery.

In that distress, while the vulgar herd was sunk in deep despair, Moses, one of their number, reminded them, that by the wisdom of his counsels they had been already rescued out of impending danger. Deserted as they were by men and gods, he told them that if they did not repose their confidence in him, as their chief by divine commission, they had no resource left. His offer was accepted. Their march began they knew not whither. Want of water was their chief distress. Worn out with fatigue they lay stretched out on the bare earth, heart-broken, ready to expire; when a troop of wild asses, returning from pasture, went up the steep ascent of a rock covered with a grove of trees. The verdure of the herbage round the place, suggested the idea of springs near at hand. Moses traced the steps of the animals, and discovered a plentiful vein of water. By this relief the fainting multitude was raised from despair. They pursued their journey for six days without intermission. On the seventh they made a halt, and having expelled the natives took possession of the country, where they built their city and dedicated their temple.

"In order to draw the bond of union closer, and to establish his own authority, Moses gave a new form of worship, and a system of religious ceremonies, the reverse of every thing known to any other age or country. Whatever is held sacred by the Romans, with the Jews is profane: and what in other nations is unlawful and impure, with them is fully established. The figure of the animal that guided them to refreshing springs is consecrated in the sanctuary of their temple[46]. In contempt of Jupiter Hammon they sacrifice a ram. The ox worshiped in Egypt for the god Apis is slain as a victim by the Jews. From the flesh of swine they abstain altogether. An animal subject to the same leprous disease that infected their whole nation, is not deemed proper food. The famine with which they were for a long time afflicted, is frequently commemorated by a solemn fast. Their bread, in memory of their having seized a quantity of grain to relieve their wants, is made without leaven. The seventh day is sacred to rest, for on that day their labours ended; and such is their natural propensity to sloth, that in consequence of it every seventh

---

[46] Conformably to this, see what Diodorus Siculus says (in the extract given from him, p. 49.): Josephus denies that the figure of an ass was consecrated in the sanctuary of the Jewish temple. But this does not invalidate the testimony of Diodorus Siculus to the contrary. For Antiochus when he subdued the Jews might have found the image of this animal in their temple; but in the time of Josephus the ass might not have been consecrated by them.

41

year is devoted to repose and sluggish inactivity. For this septennial custom some account in a different manner: they tell us that it is an institution in honour of Saturn; either because the Idæans, expelled, as has been mentioned, from the Isle of Crete, transmitted to their posterity the principles of their religious creed; or because among the seven planets that govern the universe, Saturn moves in the highest orbit, and acts with the greatest energy. It may be added that the period in which the heavenly bodies perform their revolutions is regulated by the number seven.

"These rites and ceremonies, from whatever source derived, owe their chief support to their antiquity.

They have other institutions, in themselves corrupt, impure, and even abominable; but eagerly embraced, as if their very depravity were a recommendation. The scum and refuse of other nations, renouncing the religion of their country, flocked in crowds to Jerusalem, enriching the place with gifts and offerings. Hence the wealth and grandeur of the state. Connected amongst themselves by the most obstinate and inflexible faith, the Jews extend their charity to all of their own persuasion, while towards the rest of mankind they nourish a sullen and inveterate hatred. Strangers are excluded from their tables. Unsociable to all others, they eat and lodge with one another only; and though addicted to sensuality, they admit no intercourse with women from other nations. Among themselves their passions are without restraint. Vice itself is lawful. That they may know each other by distinctive marks, they have established the practice of circumcision. All who embrace their faith, submit to the same operation. The first elements of their religion teach their proselytes to despise the gods, to abjure their country, and forget their parents, their brothers, and their children. With the Egyptians they agree in their belief of a future state; they

42

have the same notion of departed spirits, the same solicitude, and the same doctrine. With regard to the Deity their creed is different. The Egyptians worship various animals, and also symbolical representations, which are the work of man: the Jews acknowledge one God only, and him they adore in contemplation; condemning as impious idolaters all who, with perishable materials wrought into the human form, attempt to give a representation of the Deity. Their priests made use of fifes and cymbals; they were crowned with wreaths of ivy, and a vine wrought in gold was seen in their temple. Hence some have inferred that Bacchus, the conqueror of the East, was the object of their adoration. But the Jewish forms of worship have no conformity to the rites of Bacchus. The latter have their festive days which are always celebrated with mirth and carousing banquets. Those of the Jews are a gloomy ceremony, fall of absurd enthusiasm, rueful, mean, and sordid."

----

"Chæremon[47], professing to write the history of Egypt, says, that under Amenophis and his son Ramessis two hundred and fifty thousand leprous and polluted men were cast out of Egypt. Their leaders were Moses the scribe, and Josephus, who was also a sacred scribe. The Egyptian name of Moses was Tisithen, of Joseph Peteseph. These coming to Pelusium, and finding there 380,000 men left by Amenophis, which he would not admit into Egypt, making a league with them, they undertook an expedition against Egypt. Upon this Amenophis flies into Ethiopia, and his son Messenes drives out the Jews into Syria, in number about 200,000, and receives his father Amenophis out of Ethiopia. I know Lysimachus[48]

[47] Joseph, lib. i. contra Apionem.
[48] Idem.

assigns another king and another time in which Moses led the Israelites out of Egypt, and that was when Bocchoris reigned in Egypt; the nation of the Jews, being infected with leprosies and scabs and other diseases, betook themselves to the temples to beg their living, and many being tainted with the disease, there happened a dearth in Egypt. Whereupon Bocchoris consulting with the oracle of Ammon, received for answer that the leprous people were to be drowned in the sea, in sheets of lead, and the scabbed were to be carried into the wilderness; who choosing Moses for their leader, conquered that country which is now called Judæa."— Greaves Pyramidograpkia, p. 26.

# EXTRACTS FROM THE WORKS OF THE EMPEROR JULIAN RELATIVE TO THE

## EXTRACT FROM EPISTLE LI. TO THE ALEXANDRIANS

"As the founder of your city was Alexander, and your ruler and tutelar deity King Serapis, together with the virgin his associate, and the queen of all Egypt, Isis, you do not emulate a healthy city, but the diseased part dares to arrogate to itself the name of [the whole] city. By the gods, Men of Alexandria, I should be very much ashamed, if, in short, any Alexandrian should acknowledge himself to be a Galilæan.

"The ancestors of the Hebrews were formerly slaves to the Egyptians. But now, Men of Alexandria, you, the conquerors of Egypt (for Egypt was conquered by your founder), sustain a voluntary servitude to the despisers of your national dogmas, in opposition to your ancient sacred institutions. And you do not recollect your former felicity, when all Egypt had communion with the gods, and we enjoyed an abundance of good. But, tell me, what advantage has accrued to your city from those who now introduce among you a new religion? Your founder was that pious man Alexander of Macedon, who did not, by Jupiter! resemble any one of these, or any of the Hebrews, who far excelled them. Even Ptolemy, the son of Lagus, was also superior to them. As to Alexander, if he had encountered, he would have endangered even the Romans. What then did the Ptolemies, who succeeded your founder? Educating your city, like their own daughter, from her infancy, they did not bring her to maturity by the discourses of Jesus, nor did they construct the form of government, through which she is now happy, by the doctrine of the odious Galilæans.

"Thirdly: After the Romans became its masters, taking it from the bad government of the Ptolemies, Augustus visited your city, and thus addressed the citizens: 'Men of Alexandria, I acquit your city of all blame, out of regard to the great god Serapis, and also for the sake of the people, and the grandeur of the city. A third cause of my kindness to you is my friend Areus.' This Areus, the companion of Augustus Caesar, and a philosopher, was your fellow-citizen.

"The particular favours conferred on your city by the Olympic gods were, in short, such as these. Many more, not to be prolix, I omit. But those blessings which the apparent gods bestow in common every day, not on one family, nor on a single city, but on the whole world, why do you not acknowledge? Are you alone insensible of the splendour that flows from the sun? Are you alone ignorant that summer and winter are produced by him, and that all things are alone vivified and alone germinate from him? Do you not, also, perceive the great advantages that accrue to your city from the moon, from him and by him the fabricator of all things? Yet you dare not worship either of these deities; but this Jesus, whom neither you nor your fathers have seen, you think must necessarily be God the word, while him, whom from eternity every generation of mankind has seen, and sees and venerates, and by venerating lives happily, I mean the mighty sun, a living, animated, intellectual, and beneficent image of the intelligible Father, you despise. If, however, you listen to my admonitions, you will by degrees return to truth. You will not wander from the right path, if you will be guided by him, who to the twentieth year of his age pursued that road, but has now worshiped the gods for near twelve years."

## EXTRACTS FROM THE FRAGMENT OF AN ORATION OR EPISTLE ON THE DUTIES OF A PRIEST

"If any are detected behaving disorderly to their prince, they are immediately punished; but those who refuse to approach the gods, are possessed by a tribe of evil dæmons, who driving many of the atheists [i. e. of the Christians] to distraction, make them think death desirable, that they may fly up into heaven, after having forcibly dislodged their souls. Some of them prefer deserts to towns; but man, being by nature a gentle and social animal, they also are abandoned to evil dæmons, who urge them to this misanthropy; and many of them[49] have had recourse to chains and collars. Thus, on all sides, they are impelled by an evil dæmons, to whom they have voluntarily surrendered themselves, by forsaking the eternal and saviour gods.

"Statues and altars, and the preservation of the unextinguished fire, and in short all such particulars, have been established by our fathers, as symbols of the presence of the gods; not that we should believe that these symbols are gods, but that through these we should worship the gods. For since we are connected with body, it necessary that our worship of the gods should be performed in a

---

[49] i. e. The Cappadocian monks and hermits.

corporeal manner; but they are incorporeal. And they, indeed, have exhibited to us as the first of statues, that which ranks as the second genus of gods from the first, and which circularly revolves round the whole of heaven[50]. Since, however, a corporeal worship cannot even be paid to these, because they are naturally unindigent, a third kind of statues was devised in the earth, by the worship of which we render the gods propitious to us. For as those who reverence the images of kings, who are not in want of any such reverence, at the same time attract to themselves their benevolence; thus, also, those who venerate the statues of the gods, who are not in want of any thing, persuade the gods by this veneration to assist and be favourable to them. For alacrity in the performance of things in our power is a document of true sanctity; and it is very evident that he who accomplishes the former, will in a greater degree possess the latter. But he who despises things in his power, and afterwards pretends to desire impossibilities, evidently does not pursue the latter, but overlooks the former. For though divinity is not in want of any thing, it does not follow that on this account nothing is to be offered to him. For neither is he in want of celebration through the ministry of words. What then? Is it, therefore, reasonable that he should also be deprived of this? By no means. Neither, therefore, is he to be deprived of the honour which is paid him through works; which honour has been legally established, not for three or for three thousand years, but in all preceding ages, among all nations of the earth.

"But [the Galilaeans will say], O! you who have admitted into your soul every multitude of dæmons, whom, though according to you

---

[50] Meaning those divine bodies the celestial orbs, which in consequence of participating a divine life from the incorporeal powers from which they are suspended, may be very properly called secondary gods.

they are formless and unfigured, you have fashioned in a corporeal resemblance, it is not fit that honour should be paid to divinity through such works. How, then, do we not consider as wood and stones those statues which are fashioned by the hands of men? O more stupid than even stones themselves! Do you fancy that all men are to be drawn by the nose as you are drawn by execrable dæmonss, so as to think that the artificial resemblances of the gods are the gods themselves? Looking, therefore, to the resemblances of the gods, we do not think them to be either stones or wood; for neither do we think that the gods are these resemblances; since neither do we say that royal images are wood, or stone, or brass, nor that they are the kings therefore, but the images of kings. Whoever, therefore, loves his king, beholds with pleasure the image of his king; whoever loves his child is delighted with his image; and whoever loves his father surveys his image with delight. Hence, also, he who is a lover of divinity gladly surveys the statues and images of the gods; at the same time venerating and fearing with a holy dread the gods who invisibly behold him[51]. If, therefore, some

---

[51] The Catholics have employed similar arguments in defence of the reverence which they pay to the images of the men whom they call saints. But the intelligent reader need not be told, that it is one thing to venerate the images of those divine powers which proceed from the great first Cause of all things, and eternally subsist concentrated and rooted in him, and another to reverence the images of men, who when living were the disgrace of human nature. In addition to what is said by Julian on this subject, the following extract from the treatise of Sallust, on the Gods, and the World, is well worthy the attentive perusal of the reader: "A divine nature is not indigent of any thing; but the honours which we pay to the gods are performed for the sake of our advantage. And since the providence of the gods is everywhere extended, a certain habitude or fitness is all that is requisite, in order to receive their beneficent communications. But all habitude is produced through imitation and similitude.   Hence temples imitate the heavens, but altars, the earth;

one should fancy that these ought never to be corrupted, because they were once called the images of the gods, such a one appears to me to be perfectly void of intellect. For if this were admitted, it is also requisite that they should not be made by men. That, however, which is produced by a wise and good man may be corrupted by a depraved and ignorant man. But the gods which circularly revolve about the heavens, and which are living statues, fashioned by the gods themselves as resemblances of their unapparent essence, — these remain for ever. No one, therefore, should disbelieve in the gods, in consequence of seeing and hearing that some persons have behaved insolently towards statues and temples. For have there not been many who have destroyed good men, such as Socrates and Dion, and the great Empedotimus? And who, I well know, have, more than statues or temples, been taken care of by the gods. See, however, that the gods, knowing the body of these to be corruptible, have granted that it should yield and be subservient to nature, but afterwards have punished those by whom it was destroyed; which clearly happened to be the case with all the sacrilegious of our time.

"Let no one, therefore, deceive us by words, nor disturb us with respect to providential interference. For as to the prophets of the Jews, who reproach us with things of this kind, what will they say of their own temple, which has been thrice destroyed, but has not been since, even to the present time, rebuilt? I do not, however, say

---

statues resemble life, and on this account they are similar to animals. Prayers imitate that which is intellectual; but characters, superior ineffable powers. Herbs and stones resemble matter; and animals which are sacrificed, the irrational life of our souls. But, from all these, nothing happens to the gods beyond what they already possess; for what accession can be made to a divine nature? But a conjunction with our souls and the gods is by these means produced.

this as reproaching them; for I have thought of rebuilding it, after so long a period, in honour of the divinity who is invoked in it. But I have mentioned this, being willing to show, that it is not possible for any thing human to be incorruptible; and that the prophets who wrote things of this kind were delirious, and the associates of stupid old women. Nothing, however, hinders, I think, but that God may be great, and yet he may not have worthy interpreters [of his will]. But this is because they have not delivered their soul to be purified by the liberal disciplines; nor their eyes, which are profoundly closed, to be opened; nor the darkness which oppresses them to be purged away. Hence, like men who survey a great light through thick darkness, neither see purely nor genuinely, and in consequence of this do not conceive it to be a pure light, but a fire, and likewise perceiving nothing of all that surrounds it, they loudly exclaim, Be seized with horror, be afraid, fire, flame, death, a knife, a two-edged sword; expressing by many names the one noxious power of fire. Of these men, however, it is better peculiarly to observe how much inferior their teachers of the words of God are to our poets."

## AN EDICT, FORBIDDING THE CHRISTIANS TO TEACH THE LIFE-RATURE OF THE HEATHENS

"We are of opinion that proper erudition consists not in words, nor in elegant and magnificent language, but in the sane disposition of an intelligent soul, and in true opinions of good and evil, and of what is beautiful and base. Whoever, therefore, thinks one thing, and teaches another to his followers, appears to be no less destitute of erudition than he is of virtue. Even in trifles, if the mind and tongue be at variance, there is some kind of improbity. But in affairs of the greatest consequence, if a man thinks one thing, and teaches another contrary to what he thinks, in what respect does this differ from the conduct of those mean-spirited, dishonest, and abandoned traders, who generally affirm what they know to be false, in order to deceive and inveigle customers?

"All, therefore, who profess to teach, ought to possess worthy manners, and should never entertain opinions opposite to those of the public; but such especially, I think, ought to be those who instruct youth, and explain to them the works of the ancients, whether they are orators or grammarians; but particularly if they are sophists. For these last affect to be the teachers, not only of words, but of manners, and assert that political philosophy is their peculiar province. Whether, therefore, this be true or not, I shall not at present consider. I commend those who make such specious promises, and should commend them much more, if they did not falsify and contradict themselves, by thinking one thing, and teaching their scholars another. What then? Were not Homer, Hesiod, Demosthenes, Herodotus, Thucydides, Isocrates, and Lysias, the leaders of all erudition? And did not some of them consider themselves sacred to Mercury, but others to the Muses? I think, therefore, it is absurd for those who explain their works to despise the gods whom they honoured.

"I do not mean (for I think it would be absurd) that they should change their opinions for the sake of instructing youth; but I give them their option, either not to teach what they do not approve, or, if they choose to teach, first to persuade their scholars that neither Homer, nor Hesiod, nor any of those whom they expound and charge with impiety, madness, and error concerning the gods, are really such as they represent them to be. For as they receive a stipend, and are maintained by their works, if they can act with

52

such duplicity for a few drachms, they confess themselves guilty of the most sordid avarice.

"Hitherto, indeed, many causes have prevented their resorting to the temples; and the dangers that everywhere impended, were a plea for concealing the most true opinions of the gods. But now, since the gods have granted us liberty, it seems to me absurd for any to teach those things to men which they do not approve. And if they think that those writers whom they expound, and of whom they sit as interpreters, are wise, let them first zealously imitate their piety towards the gods. But if they think they have erred in their conceptions of the most honourable natures [the gods], let them go into the churches of the Galilæans, and there expound Matthew and Luke, by whom being persuaded you forbid sacrifices. I wish that your ears and your tongues were (as you express it) regenerated in those things of which I wish that myself, and all who in thought and deed are my friends, may always be partakers.

"To masters and teachers let this be a common law. But let no youths be prevented from resorting to whatever schools they please. It would be as unreasonable to exclude children, who know not yet what road to take, from the right path, as it would be to lead them by fear and with reluctance to the religious rites of their country. And though it would be just to cure such reluctance, like madness, even by force, yet let all be indulged with that disease. For I think it is requisite to instruct, and not to punish the ignorant."

# APPENDIX

## LIBANIUS'S ORATION FOR THE TEMPLES[52]

[The occasion of the oration was this. In the reign of Theodosius several heathen temples, some of them very magnificent, were pulled down and destroyed in the cities, and especially in country-places, by the monks, with the consent and connivance, as Libanius intimates, of the bishops, and without express order of the Emperor to that purpose. Of this Libanius complains, and implores the Emperor's protection, that the temples may be preserved.]

"Having already, O Emperor, often offered advice which has been approved by you, even when others have advised contrary things, I come to you now upon the same design, and with the same hopes, that now especially you will be persuaded by me. But if not, do not enemy to your interests, considering, beside other things, the great honour[53] which you have conferred upon me, and that it is not likely that he who is under so great obligations should not love his benefactor. And, for that very reason, I think it my duty to advise,

---

[52] From Dr. Lardner's Heathen Testimonies.
[53] The office of Præfectus Prætorio.

54

where I apprehend I have somewhat to offer which may be of advantage; for I have no other way of showing my gratitude to the Emperor but by orations, and the counsel delivered in them.

"I shall, indeed, appear to many to undertake a matter full of danger in pleading with you for the temples, that they may suffer no injury, as they now do. But they who have such apprehensions seem to me to be very ignorant of your true character. For I esteem it the part of an angry and severe disposition, for any one to resent the proposal of counsel which he does not approve of: but the part of a mild and gentle and equitable disposition, such as yours is, barely to reject counsel not approved of. For when it is in the power of him to whom the address is made to embrace any counsel or not, it is not reasonable to refuse a hearing which can do no harm; nor yet to resent and punish the proposal of counsel, if it appear when the only thing that induced the adviser to mention it, was a persuasion of its usefulness.

"I entreat you, therefore, O Emperor, to turn your countenance to me while I am speaking, and not to cast your eyes upon those who in many things aim to molest both you and me; forasmuch as oftentimes a look is of greater effect than all the force of truth. I would further insist, that they ought to permit me to deliver my discourse quietly and without interruption; and then, afterwards, they may do their best to confute us by what they have to say. [Here is a small breach in the Oration. But he seems to have begun his argument with an account of the origin of temples, that they were first of all erected in country places.] Men then having at first secured themselves in dens and cottages, and having there experienced the protection of the gods, they soon perceived how beneficial to mankind their favour must be: they therefore, as may be sup-, posed, erected to them statues and temples, such as they

55

could in those early times. And when they began to build cities, upon the increase of arts and sciences, there were many temples on the sides of mountains and in plains: and in every city [as they built it] next to the walls were temples and sacred edifices raised, as the beginning of the rest of the body. For from such governors they expected the greatest security: and, if you survey the whole Roman empire, you will find this to be the case every where. For in the city next to the greatest[54] there are still some temples[55], though they are deprived of their honours; a few indeed out of many, but yet it is not quite destitute. And with the aid of these gods the Romans fought and conquered their enemies; and having conquered them, they improved their condition, and made them happier than they were before their defeat; lessening their fears and making them partners in the privileges of the commonwealth. And when I was a child, he[56] led the Gallic army overthrew him that had affronted him; they having first prayed to the gods for success before they engaged. But having prevailed over him who at that time gave prosperity to the cities, judging it for his advantage to have another deity, for the building of the city which he then designed he made use of the sacred money, but made no alteration in the legal worship. The temples indeed were impoverished, but the rites were still performed there. But when the empire came to his son[57], or rather the form of empire, for the government was really in the hands of others, who from the beginning had been his masters, and to whom he vouchsafed equal power with himself: he therefore being governed by them, even when he was Emperor, was led into many wrong actions, and among others to forbid sacrifices. These

---

[54] He means Constantinople.
[55] He alludes to the ancient temples of Byzantium.
[56] Constantine.
[57] Constantius.

his cousin[58], possessed of every virtue, restored: what he did otherwise, or intended to do, I omit at present. After his death in Persia, the liberty of sacrificing remained for some time: but at the instigation of some innovators, sacrifices were forbidden by the two brothers[59], but not incense;—which state of things your law has ratified. So that we have not more reason to be uneasy for what is denied us, than to be thankful for what is allowed. You, therefore, have not ordered the temples to be shut up, nor forbidden any to frequent them: nor have you driven from the temples or the altars, fire or frankincense, or other honours of incense. But those black-garbed people[60], who eat more than elephants, and demand a large quantity of liquor from the people who send them drink for their chantings, but who hide their luxury by their pale artificial countenances,—these men, O Emperor, even whilst your law is in force, run to the temples, bringing with them wood, and stones, and iron, and when they have not these, hands and feet. Then follows a Mysian prey[61], the roofs are uncovered, walls are pulled down, images are carried off, and altars are overturned: the priests all the while must be silent upon pain of death. When they have destroyed one temple they run to another, and a third, and trophies are erected upon trophies: which are all contrary to [your] law. This is the practice in cities, but especially in the countries. And there are many enemies every where. After innumerable mischiefs have been perpetrated, the scattered multitude unites and comes together, and they require of each other an account of what they have done; and

---

[58] Julian.

[59] Valentinian and Valens.

[60] The monks.

[61] This proverbial expression took its rise from the Mysians, who, in the absence of their king Telephus, being plundered by their neighbours, made no resistance. Hence it came to be applied to any persons who were passive under injuries.

he is ashamed who cannot tell of some great injury which he has been guilty of. They, therefore, spread themselves over the country like torrents, wasting the countries together with the temples: for wherever they demolish the temple of a country, at the same time the country itself is blinded, declines, and dies. For, O Emperor, the temples are the soul of the country; they have been the first original of the buildings in the country, and they have subsisted for many ages to this time; and in them are all the husbandman's hopes, concerning men, and women, and children, and oxen, and the seeds and the plants of the ground. Wherever any country has lost its temples, that country is lost, and the hopes of the husbandmen, and with them all their alacrity: for they suppose they shall labour in vain, when they are deprived of the gods who should bless their labours; and the country not being cultivated as usual, the tribute is diminished. This being the state of things, the husbandman is impoverished, and the revenue suffers. For, be the will ever so good, impossibilities are not to be surmounted. Of such mischievous consequence are the arbitrary proceedings of those persons in the country, who say, 'they fight with the temples.' But that war is the gain of those who oppress the inhabitants: and robbing these miserable people of their goods, and what they had laid up of the fruits of the earth for their sustenance, they go off as with the spoils of those whom they have conquered. Nor are they satisfied with this, for they also seize the lands of some, saying it is sacred: and many are deprived of their paternal inheritance upon a false pretence. Thus these men riot upon other people's misfortunes, who say they worship God with fasting. And if they who are abused come to the pastor in the city, (for so they call a man who is not one of the meekest,) complaining of the injustice that has been done them, this pastor commends these, but rejects the others, as if they ought to think themselves happy that they have suffered no more. Although, O Emperor, these also are your subjects, and so much more profitable than those who injure them, as laborious men are than the idle: for they are like bees, these like drones. Moreover, if they hear of any land which has any thing that can be plundered, they cry presently, 'Such an one sacrificeth, and does abominable things, and an army ought to be sent against him.' And presently the reformers are there: for by this name they call their depredators, if I have not used too soft a word. Some of these strive to conceal themselves and deny their proceedings; and if you call them robbers, you affront them. Others glory and boast, and tell their exploits to those who are ignorant of them, and say they are more deserving than the husbandmen. Nevertheless, what is this but in time of peace to wage war with the husbandmen? For it by no means lessens these evils that they suffer from their countrymen. But it is really more grievous to suffer the things which I have mentioned in a time of quiet, from those who ought to assist them in a time of trouble. For you, O Emperor, in case of a war collect an army, give out orders, and do every thing suitable to the emergency. And the new works which you now carry on are designed as a further security against our enemies, that all may be safe in their habitations, both in the cities and in the country: and then if any enemies should attempt inroads, they may be sensible they must suffer loss rather than gain any advantage. How is it, then, that some under your government disturb others equally under your government, and permit them not to enjoy the common benefits of it? How do they not defeat your own care and providence and labours, O Emperor? How do they not fight against your law by what they do?

"But they say, 'We have only punished those who sacrifice, and thereby transgress the law, which forbids sacrifices.' O Emperor, when they say this they lie. For no one is so audacious, and so ignorant of the proceedings of the courts, as to think himself more powerful than the law. When 1 say the law, I mean the law against sacrifice». Can it be thought, that they who are not able to bear the sight of a collector s cloak, should despise the power of your government? This is what they say for themselves. And they have been often alleged to Flavian[62] himself, and never have been confuted, no not yet. For I appeal to the guardians of this law: Who has known any of those whom you have plundered to have sacrificed upon the altars, so as the law does not permit? What young or old person, what man, what woman? Who of those inhabiting the same country, and not agreeing with the sacrificers in the worship of the gods? Who of their neighbours? For envy and jealousy are common in neighbourhoods. Whence some would gladly come as an evidence if any such thing had been done: and yet no one has appeared, neither from the one nor from the other: [that is, neither from the country, nor from the neighbourhood.] Nor will there ever appear, for fear of perjury, not to say the punishment of it. Where then is the truth of this charge, when they accuse those men of sacrificing contrary to law?

"But this shall not suffice for an excuse to the Emperor. Some one therefore may say: 'They have not sacrificed.' Let it be granted. But oxen have been killed at feasts and entertainments and merry meetings. Still there is no altar to receive the blood, nor a part burned, nor do salt-cakes precede, nor any libation follow. But if some persons meeting together in some pleasant field kill a calf, or a sheep, or both, and roasting part and broiling the rest, have eat it under a shade upon the ground, I do not know that they have acted contrary to any laws. For neither have you, O Emperor, forbid these

---

[62] Bishop of Antioch

things by your law; but mentioning one thing, which ought not to be done, you have permitted every thing else. So that though they should have feasted together with all sorts of incense, they have not transgressed the law, even though in that feast they should all have sung and invoked the gods. Unless you think fit to accuse even their private method of eating, by which it has been customary for the inhabitants of several places in the country to assemble together in those [places] which are the more considerable, on holidays, and having sacrificed, to feast together. This they did whilst the law permitted them to do it. Since that, the liberty has continued for all the rest except sacrificing. When, therefore, a festival day invited them, they accepted the invitation, and with those things which might be done without offence or danger, they have honoured both the day and the place. But that they ventured to sacrifice, no one has said, nor heard, nor proved, nor been credited: nor have any of their enemies pretended to affirm it upon the ground of his own sight, nor any credible account he has received of it.

"They will further say: 'By this means some have been converted, and brought to embrace the same religious sentiments with themselves.' Be not deceived by what they say; they only pretend it, but are not convinced: for they are averse to nothing more than this, though they say the contrary. For the truth is, they have not changed the objects of their worship, but only appear to have done so. They join themselves with them in appearance, and outwardly perform the same things that they do: but when they are in a praying posture, they address to no one, or else they invoke the gods; not rightly indeed in such a place, but yet they invoke them. Wherefore as in a tragedy he who acts the part of a king is not a king, but the same person he was before he assumed the character, so every one of these keeps himself the same he was, though he seems to them to be changed. And what advantage have they by this, when the profession only is the same with theirs, but a real agreement with them is wanting? for these are things to which men ought to be persuaded, not compelled. And when a man cannot accomplish that, and yet will practise this, nothing is effected, and he may perceive the weakness of the attempt. It is said that this is not permitted by their own laws, which commend persuasion, and condemn compulsion. Why then do you run mad against the temples? When you cannot persuade, you use force. In this you evidently transgress your own laws.

"But they say: 'It is for the good of the world, and the men in it, that there should be no temples.'

Here, O Emperor, I need freedom of speech; for I fear lest I should offend. Let then any of them tell me, who have left the tongs and the hammer and the anvil, and pretend to talk of the heavens, and of them that dwell there, what rites the Romans followed, who arose from small and mean beginnings, and went on prevailing, and grew great; theirs, or these, whose are the temples and the altars, from whom they knew by the soothsayers, what they ought to do, or not to do? [Here Libanius instanceth in the successes of Agamemnon against Troy; and of Hercules before, against the same place; and some other things.] And many other wars might be mentioned, which have been successfully conducted, and after that peace obtained, by the favour and under the direction of the gods. But, what is the most considerable of all, they who seemed to despise this way of worship, have honoured it against their will. Who are they? They who have not ventured to forbid sacrifices at Rome. But if all this affair of sacrifices be a vain thing, why has not this vain thing been prohibited? And if it be hurtful likewise, why not much more? But if in the sacrifices there performed consists the stability of the empire, it ought to be reckoned beneficial to sacrifice every where; and to be allowed that the dæmonss at Rome confer greater benefits, these in the country and other cities less. This is what may be reasonably granted: for in an army all are not equal; yet in a battle the help of each one is of use: the like may be said of rowers in a vessel. So one [dæmons] defends the sceptre of Rome, another protects a city subject to it, another preserves the country and gives it felicity. Let there then be temples every where. Or let those men confess, that you are not well affected to Rome in permitting her to do things by which she suffers damage. But neither is it at Rome only that the liberty of sacrificing remains, but also in the city of Serapis[63], that great and populous city, which has a multitude of temples, by which it renders the plenty of Egypt common to all men. This [plenty] is the work of the Nile. It therefore celebrates the Nile, and persuades him to rise and overflow the fields. If those rites were not performed, when and by whom they ought, he would not do so. Which they themselves seem to be sensible of, who willingly enough abolish such things, but do not abolish these; but permit the river to enjoy his ancient rites, for the sake of the benefit he affords.

"'What then,' some will say: 'Since there is not in every country a river to do what the Nile does for the earth, there is no reason for temples in those places. Let them therefore suffer what these good people think fit.' Whom I would willingly ask this question: Whether, changing their mind, they will dare to say, Let there be an end of these things done by [or for] the Nile: let not the earth partake of his waters: let nothing be sown nor reaped: let him afford no corn, nor any other product, nor let the mud overflow the whole land, as at present. If they dare not own this, by what they

---

[63] i. e. Alexandria. The temple of Serapis was destroyed in 391.

forbear to say they confute what they do say: for they who do not affirm that the Nile ought to be deprived of his honours, confess that the honours paid to the temples are useful.

"And since they mention him[64] who spoiled the temples [of their revenues and gifts], we shall omit observing that he did not proceed to the taking away the sacrifices. But who ever suffered a greater punishment for taking away the sacred money [out of the temples], partly in what he brought upon himself; partly in what he suffered after his death, insomuch that his family destroyed one another, till there were none left? And it had been much better for him that some of his posterity should reign, than to enlarge with buildings a city of his own name: for the sake of which city itself all men still curse his memory, except those who live there in wicked luxury, because by their poverty these have their abundance.

"And since next to him they mention his son[65], and how he destroyed the temples, when they who polled them down took no less pains in destroying them, than the builders had done in raising them,—-so laborious a work was it to separate the stones cemented by the strongest bands;—since, I say, they mention these things, I will mention somewhat yet more considerable. That he indeed made presents of the temples to those who were about him, just as he might give a horse, or a slave, or a dog, or a golden cup; but they were unhappy presents to both the giver and the receivers of them: for he spent all his life in fear of the Persians, dreading all their motions as children do bugbears. Of whom, some were childless, and died miserably intestate; and others had better never have had children: with such infamy and mutual discord do they live

---

[64] Constantine
[65] Constantius.

64

together who descend from them, whilst they dwell among sacred pillars taken from the temples. To whom I think these things are owing, who knowing how to enrich themselves, have taught their children this way to happiness! And at this time their distempers carry some of them to Cilicia, needing the help of Æsculapius. But instead of obtaining relief, they meet with affronts only for the injury done to the place. How can such return without cursing the author of these evils? But let the conduct of this Emperor be such as to deserve praises living and dead; such as we know he[66] was who succeeded him; who had overturned the Persian empire if treachery had not prevented it. Nevertheless he was great in his death, for he was killed by treachery, as Achilles also was; and is applauded for that, as well as for what he did before his death. This has he from the gods, to whom he restored their rites, and honours, and temples, and altars, and blood: from whom having heard, «that he should humble the pride of Persia, and then die,' he purchased the glory of his life, taking many cities, subduing a large tract of land, teaching his pursuers to fly; and was about to receive, as all know, an embassy which would have brought the submission of the enemy. Wherefore he was pleased with his wound, and looking upon it rejoiced, and without any tears rebuked those who wept, for not thinking that a wound was better to him than any old age. So that the embassies sent after his death were all his right. And the reason why the Achemenidæ[67] for the future made use of entreaties instead of arms, was that the fear of him still possessed their minds. Such an one was he who restored to us the temples of the gods, who did things too good to be forgotten, himself above all oblivion.

---

[66] Julian.
[67] Another name for the Persians

65

"But I thought that he[68] who reigned lately would pull down and burn the temples of those who were of the opposite sentiment, as he knew how to despise the gods. But he was better than expectation, sparing the temples of the enemies, and not disdaining to run some hazards for preserving those of his own dominions, which had long since been erected with much labour and at vast expense. For if cities are to be preserved every where, and some cities outshine others by means of their temples, and these are their chief ornaments, next to the Emperor's palaces,—how is it that no care must be taken of these, nor any endeavours used to preserve them in the body of the cities?

"But it is said: 'There will be other edifices, though there should be no temples.' But I think tribute to be of importance to the treasury. Let these stand then, and be taxed. Do we think it a cruel thing to cut off a man's hand, and a small matter to pluck out the eyes of cities? And do we not lament the ruins made by earthquakes? and when there are no earthquakes, nor other accidents, shall we ourselves do what they are wont to effect? Are not the temples the possession of the Emperors as well as other things? Is it the part of wise men to sink their own goods? Does not every one suppose him to be distracted, who throws his purse into the sea? Or if the master of the ship was to cut those ropes which are of use to the ship; or if any one should order a mariner to throw away his oar,—would you think it an absurdity? and yet think it proper for a magistrate to deprive a city of such a part of it? What reason is there for destroying that, the use of which may be changed? Would it not be shameful for an army to fight against its own walls? and for a general to excite them against what they have raised with great labour; the finishing of which was a festival for those who then

---

[68] Valens.

66

reigned? Let no man think, Emperor, that this is a charge brought against you. For there lies in ruins, in the Persian borders, a temple[69], to which there is none like, as may be learned from those who saw it, so magnificent the stone work, and in compass equal to the city. Therefore in time of war the citizens thought their enemies would gain nothing by taking the town, since they could not take that likewise, as the strength of its fortifications bid defiance to all their attacks. At length, however, it was attacked, and with a fury equal to the greatest enemies, animated by the hopes of the richest plunder. I have heard it disputed,by some, in which state it was the greatest wonder; whether now that it is no more, or when it had suffered nothing of this kind, like the temple of Serapis. But that temple, so magnificent and so large, not to mention the wonderful structure of the roof, and the many brass statues, now hid in darkness out of the light of the sun, is quite perished; a lamentation to them who have seen it, a pleasure to them who never saw it. For the eyes and ears are not alike affected with these things. Or rather to those who have not seen it, it is both sorrow and pleasure: the one because of its fall, the other because their eyes never saw it. Nevertheless, if it be rightly considered, this work is not yours, but the work of a man[70] who has deceived you; a profane wretch, an enemy of the gods, base, covetous, ungrateful to the earth that received him when born, advanced without merit, and abusing his greatness, when advanced; a slave to his wife, gratifying her in any thing, and esteeming her all things, in perfect subjection to them[71] who direct these things, whose only virtue lies in wearing the habit of mourners; but especially to those of them who also weave coarse

---

[69] Probably the temple at Odessa.
[70] Probably Cynegius, the Emperor's lieutenant.
[71] The monks.

garments. This workhouse[72] deluded, imposed upon him, and misled him; [and it is said that many gods have been deceived by gods;] for they gave out, 'that the priests sacrificed, and so near them that the smoke reached their noses:' and after the manner of some simple people, they enlarge and heighten matters, and vaunt themselves as if they thought nothing was above their power. By such fiction, and contrivance, and artful stories, proper to excite displeasure, they persuaded the mildest father [of his people] among the Emperors[73]. For these were really his virtues, humanity, tenderness, compassion, mildness, equity, who had rather save than destroy. But there were those who gave lister counsel; that if such a thing had been done, the attempt should be punished, and care taken to prevent the like for time to come. Yet he who thought he ought to have a Cadmean victory, carried on his conquest. But after he had taken his own pleasures, he should have provided for his people, and not have desired to appear great to those who shun the labours of the country, and converse in the mountains[74], as they say, with the Maker of all things. But let your actions appear excellent and praiseworthy to all men. There are at this time many, so far friends as to receive and empty your treasures, and to whom your empire is dearer than their own souls; but when the time comes that good counsel and real services are wanted, they have no concern upon them but to take care of themselves; and if any one comes to them, and inquires what this means, they excuse themselves as free from all fault. They disown what they have done, or pretend 'that they have obeyed the Emperor's order; and if there is any blame, he must see to it.' Such things they say, when it is they who are found guilty, who can give no account of their

---

[72] The monastery.

[73] Probably Valens.

[74] He refers to the monks near Antioch,

actions. For what account can be given of such mischiefs? These men before others deny this to be their own work. But when they address you alone, without witnesses, they say, 'they have been in this war serving your family.' They would deliver your house from those who by land and sea endeavour to defend your person; than which there is nothing greater you can receive from them. For these men, under the name of friends and protectors, telling stories of those by whom they say they have been injured, improve your credulity into an occasion of doing more mischief.

"But I return to them, to demonstrate their injustice by what they have said: Say then, for what reason you destroyed that great temple? Not because the Emperor approved the doing it. They who pull down a temple have done no wrong if the Emperor has ordered it to be done. Therefore they who pulled it down did not do wrong by doing what the Emperor approved of. But he who does that which is not approved by the Emperor, does Wrong; does he not? You, then, are the men who have nothing of this to say for what you have done. Tell me why this temple of Fortune is safe? and the temple of Jupiter, and of Minerva, and of Bacchus? Is it because you would have them remain? No, but because no one has given you power over them; which, nevertheless, you have assumed against those which you have destroyed. How, then, are you not liable to punishment? or how can you pretend that what you have done is right, when the sufferers have done no wrong? Of which charge there would have been some appearance, if you, O Emperor, had published an edict to their purpose: 'Let no man within my empire believe in the gods, nor worship them, nor ask any good thing of them, neither for himself, nor for his children, unless it be done in silence and privately: but let all present themselves at the places where I worship, and join in the rites there

69

performed. And let them offer the same prayers which they do, and bow the head at the hand of him who directs the multitude. Whoever transgresses this law, shall be put to death.' It was easy for you to publish such a law as this; but you have not done it; nor have you in this matter laid a yoke upon the souls of men. But though you think one way better than the other, yet you do not judge that other to be an impiety, for which a man may be justly punished. Nor have you excluded those of that sentiment from honours, but have conferred upon them the highest offices, and have given them access to your table, to eat and drink with you. This you have done formerly, and at this time; beside others, you have associated to yourself (thinking it advantageous to your government) a man, who swears by the gods, both before others, and before yourself: and you are not offended at it; nor do you think yourself injured by those oaths: nor do you account him a wicked man who placeth his best hopes in the gods. When, therefore, you do not reject us, as neither did he who subdued the Persians by arms reject those of his subjects who differed from him in this matter, what pretence have these to reject us?

How can these men reject their fellow-subjects, differing from them in this matter? By what right do they make these incursions? How do they seize other men's goods with the indignation of the countries? How do they destroy some things, and carry off others? adding to the injury of their actions the insolence of glorying in them. We, O Emperor, if you approve and permit these things, will bear them; not without grief indeed; but yet we will show that we have learned to obey. But if you give them no power, and yet they come and invade our small remaining substance, or our walls: Know, that the owners of the countries will defend themselves."

# EXTRACTS FROM BINGHAM'S ANTIQUITIES OF THE CHRISTIAN CHURCH[75]

## OF THE NAMES OF REPROACH WHICH THE JEWS, INFIDELS, AND HERETICS CAST UPON THE CHRISTIANS

"Besides the names already spoken of, there were some other reproachful names cast upon them by their adversaries, which it will not be improper here to mention. The first of these was Nazarens, a name of reproach given them first by the Jews, by whom they are styled the sect of the Nazarens, Acts xxiv. 5. There was indeed a particular heresy, who called themselves [—Greek—]: and Epiphanius[76] thinks the Jews had a more especial spite at them, because they were a sort of Jewish apostates, who kept circumcision and the Mosaical rites together with the Christian religion: and therefore, he says, they were used to curse and anathematize them three times a day, morning, noon, and evening, when they met in their synagogues to pray, in this direful form of execration,' [—

---

[75] The edition from which these Extracts are taken it in one vol. 8vo, London, 1708, and begins at p. 13.
[76] Epiphan. Haer. 29. n. 9.

71

Greek—], 'Send thy curse, O God, upon the Nazarens.' But St. Jerome[77] says this was levelled at Christians in general, whom they thus anathematized under the name of Nazarens. And this seems most probable, because both as St. Jerome[78] and Epiphanius himself[79] observe, the Jews termed all Christians by way of reproach, Nazarens. And the Gentiles took it from the Jews, as appears from that of Datianus the praetor in Prudentius[80], where speaking to the Christians he gives them the name of Nazarens. Some[81] think the Christians at first were very free to own this name, and esteemed it no reproach, till such time as the heresy of the Nazarens broke out, and then in detestation of that heresy they forsook that name, and called themselves Christians. Acts xi. 26. But whether this be said according to the exact rules of chronology, I leave those that are better skilled to determine.

Another name of reproach was that of Galilæans, which was Julian's ordinary style, whenever he spake of Christ or Christians. Thus in his Dialogue with old Maris a blind Christian bishop, mentioned by Sozomen[82], he told him by way of scoff, "Thy Galilæan God will not cure thee." And again, in his epistle[83] to

---

[77] Hieron. Com. in Esa. xlix. t 5. p. 178. Ter per tingulos dies sub nomine Nazaienorum maledicunt in synagogis suis.

[78] Id. de loc. Hebr. t. 3. p. 289. Nos apnd veterei» quasi opprobrio Nazaraei dicebamur, quos nunc Christianos vocant.

[79] Epiphan. ibid.

[80] Prudent. — — — —-]. Carm. 5. de S. Vincent.
    Vos Nazareni assistite,
    Rudemque ritum spernite.
  Id. Hymno 9. de Rom. Mart.

[81] Junius, Parallel, lib. 1. c. 8. Godwyn, Jew. Rites, lib. 1. c. 8.

[82] Sozom. lib. 5. c. 4.

[83] A p. Sozom. lib. 5. c. 16.
  (v) Socrat. lib. 3. c. 12.

Arsacius high-priest of Galatia, "The Galilæans maintain their own poor and ours also." The like may be observed in Socrates(v), Theodoret (vi), Chrysostom[84], and Gregory Nazianzen[85], who adds, that he not only called them Galilæans himself, but made a law that no one should call them by any other name; thinking thereby to abolish the name of Christians.

They also called them Atheists, and their religion the Atheism or Impiety, because they derided the worship of the heathen gods. Dio[86] says, Acilius Glabrio was put to death for atheism, meaning the Christian religion. And the Christian apologists, Athenagoras[87] Justin Martyr(v), Arnobius(vi), and others, reckon this among the crimes which the heathens usually lay to their charge. Eusebius says(vii) the name was become so common, that when the persecuting magistrates would oblige a Christian to renounce his religion, they bade him abjure it in this form, by saying among other things, [—Greek—] 'Confusion to the atheists, Away with the impious,' meaning the Christians.

To this they added the name of Greeks and Impostors. Which is noted by St. Jerome(viii) who says wheresoever they saw a Christian, they would presently cry out, '[—Greek—], 'Behold a Grecian impostor.' This was the character which the Jews gave our

---

(vi) Theodor. lib. 3. c 7. & 31.
[84] Chrys. Horn. 63. torn. 5.
[85] Naz. i. Invectiv.
[86] Dio in Domitian.
[87] Athen. Legat. pro Christ.
  (v) Just. Apol. i. p. 47.
  (vi) Arnob. lib. i.
  (vii) Euseb. lib. iv. c. 15.
  (viii) Hieron. Ep. 10. ad Furiara. Ubicunque viderint

Saviour, [—Greek—]' that deceiver[88], Matt, xxvii. 63. And Justin Martyr[89] says, they endeavoured to propagate it to posterity, sending their apostles or emissaries from Jerusalem to all the synagogues in the world, to bid them beware of a certain impious, lawless sect, lately risen up under one Jesus, a Galilæan impostor. Hence Lucian[90] took occasion in his blasphemous raillery to style him The crucified sophister. And Celsus[91] commonly gives him and his followers the name of [—Greek—] 'deceivers.' So Asclepiades the judge in Prudentius compliments them with the appellation of sophisters; and Ulpian(v) proscribes them in a law by the name of impostors.

The reason why they added the name of Greeks to that of impostors, was (as learned men[92] conjecture) because many of the Christian philosophers took upon them the Grecian or philosophic habit, which was the [—Greek—] or pallium: whence the Greeks were called Pallitati, as the Romans were called Togati, or Gens togata, from their proper habit, which was the toga. Now it being some offence to the Romans to see the Christians quit the Roman gown, to wear the Grecian cloak; they thence took occasion, to mock and deride them with the scurrilous names of Greeks, and Grecian impostors. Tertullian s book de Pallio was written to show the spiteful malice of this foolish objection.

---

[88] Christianum, statim illud de Trivio, [—Greek—] vocant Impostorem.
[89] Justin. Dial. c. Tryph. p. 335.
[90] Lucian. Peregrin.
[91] Cels. ap. Orig. lib. i. et lib. 6.
   (v) Prudent. [—Greek—]. Carm. 9. de Romano Marty. Quis hos Sophistas error invexit novus, &c.
   (vi) Digest, lib. 50. tit. 13. c 1. Si incantavit, si inprecatus est, si (ut vulgari verbo Impostoruxn utar) si exorcisavit
[92] Kortholt de Morib. Christian, c. 3. p. 23. Baron an. 56. n. 11.

But the heathens went one step further in their malice; and because our Saviour and his followers did many miracles, which they imputed to evil arts and the power of magic, they therefore generally declaimed against them as magicians, and under that character exposed them to the fury of the vulgar. Celsus[93] and others pretended that our Saviour studied magic in Egypt: and St. Austin[94] says, it was generally believed among the heathens, that he wrote some books about magic too, which he delivered to Peter and Paul for the use of his disciples. Hence it was that Suetonius[95] speaking in the language of his party, calls the Christians Genus hominum superstionis maleficae, 'the men of the magical superstition.' As Asclepiades the judge in Prudentius[96] styles St. Romanus the martyr, Arch-magician.

And St. Ambrose observes in the Passion of St. Agnes[97] how the people cried out against her, 'Away with the sorceress! Away with the enchanter! 'Nothing being more common than to term all Christians, especially such as wrought miracles, by the odious name of sorcerers and magicians.'

The New Superstition was another name of reproach for the Christian religion. Suetonius gives it that title[98], and Pliny and

---

[93] Origen. cont. Cels. lib. 2. Arrobius, lib. 1. p. 36.
[94] Aug. de Consensu Evang. lib. 1. c. 9.
[95] Sueton. Neron. c. 16.
[96] Prudent. Hymn. 9. de S. Romano. Quousque tandem su m m us hic nobis Magus illudit.
[97] Ambr. Serm. 90. in S. Agnen. Tolle Magam! Tolle Maleticam!
[98] See Kortholt de Morib. Christ, c. 4.
    (v) Sueton. Nero. c. 16.
    (vi) Plin. lib. 10. ep. 97. Nihil aliud inveni, quam superstitionem pravam et immodicara. Tacit. Annal. 15. c.
    44. Exitiabilis superstitio.

Tacitus add to it(v) the opprobrious terms of wicked and unreasonable superstition. By which name also Nero triumphed over it in his trophies which he set up at Rome, when he had harassed the Christians with a most severe persecution. He gloried that he had purged the country of robbers, and those that obtruded and inculcated the new superstition[99] upon mankind. By this, there can be no doubt he meant the Christians, whose religion is called the superstition in other inscriptions of the like nature. See that of Diocletian cited in Baronius, Ann. 304. from Occo. "Superstitione Christianorum ubique deleta," &c.

Not much unlike this was that other name which Porphyry[100] and some others give it, when they call it the barbarous, new, and strange religion. In the acts of the famous martyrs of Lyons, who suffered under Antoninus Pius, the heathens scornfully insult it with this character. For having burnt the martyrs to ashes, and scattered their remains into the river Rhone, they said, they did it 'to cut off their hopes of a resurrection, upon the strength of which they sought to obtrude[101] the new and strange religion upon mankind. But now let us see whether they will rise again, and whether their God can help and deliver them out of our hands.'

Celsus gives them the name of Sibyllists[102], because the Christians in their disputes with the heathens sometimes made use of the authority of Sibylla their own prophetess against them; whose writing they urged with so much advantage to the Christian cause,

---

[99] Inscript. Antiq. ad Calcem Sueton. Oxon. NERONI. CLAUD. CAIS. AUG. PONT. MAX. OB. PROVING. LATRONIB. ET. HIS. QUI. NOVAM. GENERI. HUM. SUPERSTITION. INCULCAB. PURGAT.
[100] Ap. Euseb. Hist Eccl, lib* 6, c 19, [—Greek—]
[101] Act. Mart. Lugd. ap. Euseb. lib. 5. c. 1. [—Greek—]
[102] Origen. c. Cels. lib. 5. p. 272.

and prejudice to the heathen, that Justin Martyr[103] says, the Roman governors made it death for any one to read them, or Hystaspes, or the writings of the prophets.

They also reproached them with the appellation of [−Greek−], 'self-murderers,' because they readily offered themselves up to martyrdom, and cheerfully underwent any violent death, which the heathens could inflict upon them. With what eagerness they courted death, we learn not only from the Christian writers[104] themselves, but from the testimonies of the heathens[105] concerning them. Lucian[106] says they not only despised death, but many of them voluntarily offered themselves to it, out of a persuasion that they should be made immortal and live forever. This he reckons folly, and therefore gives them the name of [−Greek−], 'The miserable wretches, that threw away their lives,' In which sense Porphyry[107] also styles, the Christian religion, [−Greek−] the barbarous boldness.' As Arrjus Antoninus[108] terms the professors of it, [−Greek−], The stupid wretches, that had such a mind to die; and the heathen in Minucius(v), homines deploratae ac desperate factionis, 'the men of the forlorn and desperate faction.' All which agrees with the name Biothanati, or Biaeothanati, as Baronius(vi) understands it* Though it may signify not only self-murderers, but (as a learned critic(xii) notes) men that expect to live after death. In

---

103 Just Apol. 2. p. 82.
104 See these collected in Pearson, Vind. Ignat. Par. 2. c. 9. p. 384.
105 Arrius Antonin. ap. Tertul. ad Scap. c. 4. Tiberias, in Joh. Malela Chronic.
106 Lucian. de Mort Peregrin.
107 Porphyr. ap. Euseb. Hist Eccl. 1. 6. c 19.
108 Tertul. ibid.
  (v) Minuc. Octav. p. 25.
  (vi) Baron, an. 138. n. 5.
  (vii) Suicer. Thesaur. Ecclesiast 1.1. p. 690.

which sense the heathens probably might use it likewise to ridicule the Christian doctrine of the resurrection; on which, they knew, all their fearless and undaunted courage was founded. For so the same heathen in Minucius endeavours to expose at once both their resolution and their belief: "O strange folly, and incredible madness!" says he; "they despise all present torments, and yet fear those that are future and uncertain: they are afraid of dying after death, but in the mean time do not fear to die. So vainly do they flatter themselves, and allay their fears, with the hopes of some reviving comforts after death." For one of these reasons then they gave them the name of Biothanati, which word expressly occurs in some of the acts of the ancient martyrs. Baronius observes[109] out of Bede's Martyrology, that when the seven sons of Symphorosa were martyred under Hadrian, their bodies were all cast into one pit together, which the temple-priests named from them, Ad Septem Biothanatos, 'The grave of the seven Biothanati.'

For the same reasons they gave them the names of Parabolarii and Desperati, 'The bold and desperate men.' The Parabolarii, or Parabolani among the Romans were those bold adventurous men, who hired out themselves to fight with wild beasts upon the stage or amphitheatre, whence they had also the name of Bestiarii, and Confectores. Now because the Christians were put to fight for their lives in the same manner, and they rather chose to do it than deny their religion, they therefore got the name of Paraboli and Parabolani: which, though it was intended as a name of reproach and mockery, yet the Christians were not unwilling to take to themselves, being one of the truest characters that the heathens ever gave them. And therefore they sometimes gave themselves this name by way of allusion to the Roman Paraboli. As in the Passion

---

[109] Baron, an. 138. n. 5.

of Abdo and Senne[110] in the time of Valerian, the martyrs who were exposed to be devoured by wild beasts in the amphitheatre, are said to enter, 'ut audacissimi Parabolani,' as most resolute champions, that despised their own lives for their religion's sake. But the other name of Desperati they rejected as a calumny, retorting it back upon their adversaries, who more justly deserved it. "Those," says Lactantius[111], "who set a value upon their faith, and will not deny their God, they first torment and butcher with all their might, and then call them desperados, because they will not spare their bodies: as if any thing could be more desperate, than to torture and tear in pieces those whom you cannot but know to be innocent."

Tertullian mentions another name, which was likewise occasioned by their sufferings. The martyrs which were burnt alive, were usually tied to a board or stake of about six foot long, which the Romans called semaxis; and then they were surrounded or covered with faggots of small wood, which they called sarmenia. From this their punishment, the heathens, who turned every thing into mockery, gave all Christians the despiteful name of Sarmentitii and Semaxii[112].

The heathen in Minucius[113] takes occasion also to reproach them under the name of the sculking generation, or the men that loved to prate in corners and the dark. The ground of which scurrilous reflection was only this, that they were forced to hold their religious

---

[110] Acta Abdon. et Sennes ap. Suicer.

[111] Lact. Instil, lib. 5. c. 9. Desperates vocant, quia corpori suo minime parcunt, &c.

[112] Tertul. Apol. t, 50. Licet nunc Sarmentitios et Semaxios appelletis, quia ad stipitem dimidii axis re-vincti, sarmentorum ambitu exurimur.

[113] Minuc. Octav. p. 25. Latebrosa et lucifugax natio, in publicum muta, in angulis garrula.

assemblies in the night to avoid the fury of the persecutions. Which Celsus[114] himself owns, though otherwise prone enough to load them with hard names and odious reflections.

The same heathen in Minucius gives them one scurrilous name more, which it is not very easy to guess the meaning of. He calls them Plautinians[115],—homines Plautinæ prosapiæ. Rigaltius[116] takes it for a ridicule upon the poverty and simplicity of the Christians, whom the heathens commonly represented as a company of poor ignorant mechanics, bakers, tailors, and the like; men of the same quality with Plautus, who, as St. Jerome[117] observes, was so poor, that at a time of famine he was forced to hire out himself to a baker to grind at his mill, during which time he wrote three of his Plays in the intervals of his labour. Such sort of men Coecilius says the Christians were; and therefore he styles Octavius in the dialogue, homo Plautinæ prosapiæ et pistorum præcipuus, 'a Plautinian, a chief man among the illiterate bakers,' but no philosopher. The same reflection is often made by Celsus. "You shall see," says he[118], "weavers, tailors, fullers, and the most illiterate and rustic fellows, who dare not speak a word before wise men, when they can get a company of children and silly women together, set up to teach strange paradoxes amongst them." "This is one of their rules," says he again[119],—"Let no man that is learned, wise, or prudent come

---

[114] Origen. c. Cel. lib. 1. p. 5.
[115] Minuc. p. 37. Quid ad hæc audet Octavius homo Plautinæ Prosapiæ, ut Pistorum præcipuus ita postremus Philosophorum?
[116] Rigalt. in loc.
[117] Hieron. Chronic, an. 1. Olymp. 145.
[118] Origen. c Cels. lib. 3. p. 144.
[119] Origen. c. Cels. lib. 3. p. 137. f See the preceding translation of Celsus, p. 19. f Eulog. ap. Phot. Cod. 280. § Facian. Ep. 2. ad Sympronian. ‖ Ep. Legat. Schismat ad suos in Epheso in Act. Con. Ephes. Con. t S. p. 746. f Sozora, lib, 6. c. 21.

among us; but if any be unlearned, or a child, or an ideot, let him freely come. So they openly declare, that none but fools and sots, and such as want sense, slaves, women, and children, are fit disciples for the God they worship."

Nor was it only the heathens that thus reviled them, but commonly every perverse sect among the Christians had some reproachful name to cast upon them. The Novatian party called them Cornelieans because they communicated with Cornelius bishop of Rome, rather than with Novatianus his antagonist. They also termed them Apostates, Capitolins, Synedrians, because they charitably decreed in their synods to receive apostates, and such as went to the Capitol to sacrifice, into their communion again upon their sincere repentance. The Nestorians(v) termed the orthodox Cyrillians; and the Arians(vi) called them Eustathians and Paulinions, from Eustathius and Paulin us bishops of Antioch. As also Homousians, because they kept to the doctrine of the [— Greek—], which declared the Son of God to be of the same substance with the Father. The author of the Opus Imperfection on St. Matthew, under the name of Chrysostom[120], styles them expressly, Hæresis Homoousianorum,' the heresy of the Homoousians.' And so Serapion in his conflict with Arnobius[121] calls them Homousianates,which the printed copy reads corruptly Homuncionates, which was a name for the Nestorians.

The Cataphrygians or Montanists commonly called the orthodox [—Greek—], 'carnal'; because they rejected the prophecies and pretexted inspirations of Montanus, and would not receive his rigid laws about fasting, nor abstain from second marriages, and observe

---

[120] Opus Imperf. Horn. 48.
[121] Conflict. Arnob. et Serap. ad cakem Irenæi, p. 519.

four Lents in a year, &c. This was Tertullian's ordinary compliment to the Christians in all his books[122] written after he was fallen into the errors of Montanus. He calls his own party the spiritual, and the orthodox the carnal: and some of his books[123] are expressly entitled, Adversus Psychicos. Clemens Alexandrinus[124] observes, the same reproach was also used by other heretics beside the Montanists. And it appears from Irenæus, that this was an ancient calumny of the Valentinîans, who styled themselves the spiritual and the perfect, and the orthodox the secular and carnal[125], who had need of abstinence and good works, which were not necessary for them that were perfect.

The Millenaries styled them Allegorists, because they expounded the prophecy of the saints reigning a thousand years with Christ, (Rev. xx. 4.) to a mystical and allegorical sense. Whence Euseubius[126] observes of Nepos the Egyptian bishop, who wrote for the Millenium, that he entitled his book, [−Greek−], 'A confutation of the Allegorists.'

Aetius the Arian gives them the abusive name of [−Greek−]; by which he seems to intimate, that their religion was but temporary, and would shortly have an end; whereas the character was much more applicable to the Arians themselves, whose faith was so lately sprung up in the world; as the author of the dialogues de Trinitate,

---

[122] Tertul. adv. Prax. c. 1. Nos quidem agnitio Paracleti disjunxit à Psychicis. Id. de Monogam. c. 1. Haeretici nuptias auferunt, Psychici ingerunt. See also c. 11. and 16.

[123] De Jejuniis adv. Psychicos.   De Pudicitia, &c.

[124] Clem. Alex. Strom, lib. 4. p. 511.

[125] Iren. lib. 1. c 1. p. 29. Nobis quidem, quos Psychicos vocant, et de sæculo esse dicunt, necessarian) continentiam, &c.

[126] Euseb. lib. 7. c. 24.

under the name of Athanasius, who confutes Aetius[127], justly retorts upon him.

The Manichees, as they gave themselves the most glorious names of Electi, Macarii, Catharistæ, mentioned by St. Austin[128]; so they reproached the Catholics with the most contemptible name of Simplices, 'ideots,' which is the term that Manichæus himself used in his dispute[129] with Archelaus, the Mesopotamian bishop, styling the Christian teachers, Simpliciorum magistri, 'guides of the simple;' because they could not relish his execrable doctrine concerning two principles of good and evil.

The Apollinarians were no less injurious to the Catholics, in fixing on them the odious name of Anthropolatræ, 'man-worshippers'; because they maintained that Christ was a perfect man, and had a reasonable soul and body, of the same nature with ours; which Apollinarius denied. Gregory Nazianzen[130] takes notice of this abuse, and sharply replies to it; telling the Apollinarians, that they themselves much better deserved the name of Sarcolatræ, 'flesh-worshippers': for if Christ had no human soul, they must be concluded to worship his flesh only.

The Origenians, who denied the truth of the resurrection, and asserted that men should have only aerial and spiritual bodies in the next world, made jests upon the Catholics, because they maintained the contrary, that our bodies should be the same individual bodies, and of the same nature that they are now, with flesh and bones, and all the members in the same form and

---

[127] Athan. Dial. 2. de Trinit. t. 2. p. 193.
[128] Aug. de Hær. c. 46.
[129] Archel. Disp. adv. Manichaeum adcalcem Sozomen. Ed. Vales, p. 197.
[130] Naz. Ep. 1. ad Cledon.

structure, only altered in quality, not in substance. For this they gave them the opprobrious names of Simplices and Philosarcæ[131], 'ideots' and 'lovers of the flesh'; Carnei, Animales, Jumenta, 'carnal, sensual, animals'; Lutei, 'earthy', Pilosiotæ[132], which Erasmus's edition reads corruptly Pelusiotæ, instead of Pilonotæ; which seems to be a name formed from pili, (hair); because the Catholics asserted, that the body would rise perfect in all its parts, even with the hair itself to beautify and adorn it.

But of all others the Luciferians gave the church the rudest language; styling her the brothel-house, and synagogue of Antichrist and Satan; because she allowed those bishops to retain their honour and places, who were cajoled by the Arians to subscribe the fraudulent confession of the Council of Ariminum. The Luciferian in St. Jerome runs out in this manner against the church; and St. Jerome says, he spake but the sense of the whole party, for this was the ordinary style and language of all the rest.— Hieron. Dial. adv. Lucifer, t. ii. p. 135."

Thus far Bingham: to whose extracts may appropriately be added, what the Emperor Julian says reproachfully of the Christians, in the fragments which Cyril has preserved of his Treatise against them. "You do not take notice (says he) whether any mention is made by the Jews of holiness; but you emulate their rage and their bitterness, overturning temples and altars, and cutting the throats, not only of those who remain firm in paternal institutes, but also of those

---

[131] Hieron. Ep. 61. ad Pammach. t. 2. p. 171. Nos Simplices et Philosarcas dicere, quod eadem ossa, et sanguis, et caro, id est, vultus et membra, totiusque compago corporis resurgat in novissima die.
[132] Id. Ep. 65, ad Pam. et Ocean, de Error. Orig. p. 192. Pelusiotas (leg. Pilosiotas) nos appellant, et Luteos, Animalesque, et Cameos, quod non recipiamus ea quae Spiritus sunt.

heretics who are equally erroneous with yourselves, and who do not lament a dead body [i. e. the body of Christ] in the same manner as you do[133]. For neither Jesus nor Paul exhorted you to act in this manner. But the reason is, that neither did they expect that you would ever arrive at the power which you have obtained. For they were satisfied if they could deceive maidservants and slaves, and through these married women, and such men as Cornelius and Sergius; among whom if you can mention one that was at that time an illustrious character, (and these things were transacted under the reign of Tiberius or Claudius) believe that I am a liar in all things[134]."

THE END

---

[133] Julian here alludes to the contests between the Arians and Trinitarians.
[134] Vid. Cyril, apud Spanh.